STRENGTH FOR THE STORM

Spiritual lessons –
John Sung and oth
which prepared t

TRANSLATED BY
ARTHUR REYNOLDS

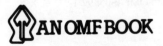

AN OMF BOOK

© OVERSEAS MISSIONARY FELLOWSHIP
(formerly China Inland Mission)
Published by Overseas Missionary Fellowship (IHQ) Ltd.,
2 Cluny Road, Singapore 1025,
Republic of Singapore

First published 1988
Reprinted 1989

OMF BOOKS are distributed by
OMF, 404 South Church Street, Robesonia, PA 19551, USA
OMF, Belmont, The Vine, Sevenoaks, Kent, TN13 3TZ, UK
OMF, P O Box 849, Epping, NSW 2121, Australia
OMF, 1058 Avenue Road, Toronto, Ontario M5N 2C6, Canada
OMF, P O Box 10159 Balmoral, Auckland, New Zealand
OMF, P O Box 41, Kenilworth 7745, South Africa
and other OMF offices.

OMF ISBN 9971-972-62-X

Printed in Singapore
SW 3K/12/89

Contents

Contents

FOREWORD

180 years ago Robert Morrison arrived as the first Protestant missionary to China. As he was about to board ship in England for that historic voyage, he was ridiculed: "Young man, do you think you can influence such a great and ancient empire?" Little could the pioneer missionary have realized how prophetic his reply would prove to be: "No, Sir, but God can!"

In twelve short years Morrison not only mastered the language and compiled the first Chinese-English dictionary, but he also completed a translation of the entire Bible into Chinese. That proved to be the secret of his impact on China. Long ago Isaiah declared that when God's Word goes out, it will not return empty, but will accomplish what He desires and achieve the purpose for which He sent it. 52 million believers in China today (according to David Barrett's latest study) stand as irrefutable evidence and testimony to the power of God's Word; not to speak of 3250 churches in Hong Kong and Taiwan, 1500 Chinese churches in Southeast Asia and 830 in North America. As stated at a recent China Consultation in Washington DC, "Though gnarled and often faltering missionary hands planted the acorn of God's Word in China, today it has grown into a sturdy oak."

The initial period of Protestant missions (1807–1865) saw a small missionary contingent establish footholds in the major coastal cities and among overseas Chinese communities in Southeast Asia. Bible translation and the production of Christian literature was an important aspect of their early efforts in evangelism.

Then followed the inland period (1865–1905)

when a rapidly expanding missionary movement, supported by more and more Chinese colleagues, carried the gospel into the heartland of China. During this time every inland province was entered. At the same time Christian schools were being established in areas where the church was more advanced and potential indigenous leadership for the church in China began to emerge.

The Boxer Uprising in 1900, followed by the fall of the Qing Dynasty a decade later, led to the accelerated emergence of strong indigenous leadership. A new spirit of national consciousness found varied expression in the May Fourth Movement and the birth pangs of the Chinese Republic. It was during the incredibly tempestuous opening decades of the 20th century that all the Christian leaders whose messages Arthur Reynolds has painstakingly made available for the English reader were born.

John Stott speaks of five essential ingredients that make leadership Christian: vision, industry, perseverance, service and discipline. These five important distinctives are marks of these Chinese evangelical leaders God raised up earlier this century to make Christianity the amazing indigenous expression we see today. There were of course many other outstanding men of God, pastors, evangelists, teachers and writers, who were used in equally significant ways during this same period of time. I am sure that it is no reflection on the influence or effectiveness of their ministry that samples of the message they proclaimed have not been included in Arthur Reynold's collection.

Some readers who are accustomed to, or are looking for, a more expositional style of preaching may be disappointed not to find their expectation fully satisfied in the more typical Chinese style illustrated in this book. None, however, will fail to rejoice in the consistent exaltation of Christ and the call for an application of biblical truth in individual, family and church life. In both aspects we can benefit greatly ourselves today.

"Therefore, since we are surrounded by such a great cloud of witnesses, let us throw off everything that hinders and the sin that so easily entangles, and let us run with perseverance the race marked out for us. Let us fix our eyes on Jesus, the author and perfector of our faith, who for the joy set before him endured the cross, scorning its shame, and sat down at the right hand of the throne of God. Consider him who endured such opposition from sinful men, so that you will not grow weary and lose heart." Hebrews 12: 1–3.

James H Taylor III

TRANSLATOR'S INTRODUCTION

BY THEIR STURDY faith and indomitable courage the churches in China, like the church of the Thessalonians, have become a pattern for believers beyond their boundaries. From the time of the Boxer Rising in 1900, if not much earlier, the Christians in China have learned to live with persecution. No period of testing has proved fiercer, longer lasting or more widespread that that which began before mid-century, when one upheaval followed another. More recently the situation for the Christian community has somewhat eased. But there is still a long way to go.

Survival and Growth
Humanly speaking, no one could have had any grounds for expecting the church to survive. In point of fact the churches have steadily grown and, surprisingly to many, this growth has embraced young as well as old. Surges of heightened spiritual life are not unusual. No one can say how many Christians there are today. Estimates vary widely, but they can certainly be numbered in millions.

And it is not just a question of numbers. Who can fail to be impressed by the high calibre of the Christians in China? The evidence of robust Christian faith and contagious witness, along with love of God and His Word, is strong and reliable.

How did this come about? What has enabled the Christians to endure in this way? What is the source of their zeal and faith and courage? How have they overcome? What are the reasons for this church's power of endurance?

We must begin, of course, with the sovereignty of God and with His presence and protection. "On this rock," said Jesus, "I will build my church, and the gates of Hades will not overcome it" (Matt. 16:18).

Pioneer missionaries
Obviously the existence of so many centres of witness in the interior was due, in the first place, to the persevering and sacrificial work of pioneer missionaries. These men and women could say, as the apostle Paul did, "I consider my life worth nothing to me if only I may finish the race and complete the task the Lord Jesus has given me — the task of testifying the gospel of God's grace" (Acts 20:24).

It happens that among those early missionaries were my wife's grandparents, Adam Grainger and his wife, who came from Scotland. At the turn of the century travel in China was so difficult that when their children went off to school at the other end of the country at about the age of six, they did not see their parents again for four years. Even in our own days as missionaries children had to be separated from their parents — unless some special provision was made — for over three years from the age of eight or so. In that way many children of missionaries have shared deeply in the heartache and sacrifices of this work of pioneering and propagating the gospel.

The Secret of the Churches' Continuity
Apart from the presence of the One who walks among the churches, what is the secret of the maintenance of the Chinese Church's spiritual life? To me at least the main answer is undoubtedly the high calibre of Christian leadership.

Forty years or so ago, two levels of opportunity and influence existed among Christian leaders in

China. On one level were the local leaders of smaller churches in the numerous towns and larger villages. At that time hardly a town anywhere in all the main provinces was without at least a small group of Christian believers. Then on the other level we can identify a handful of men who by any standard must be reckoned as quite outstanding, if not unique.

Holding the Fort

The role of local leaders and workers assumes great importance in areas where groups of Christians are largely cut off from each other. I observed this situation during my travels of the 1930s and 40s both to the fringe of the Mongolian desert and also over much of China's great north-west. At one stage I was asked to spend several months visiting isolated Christian groups in the predominantly Muslim province of Qinghai and the Tibetan border region. I travelled on horseback in the company of a Tibetan-speaking Swedish colleague, Brother Cronhielm.

How happy those believers were when Bible teachers from outside could spend perhaps a week with them to preach the gospel and to teach the Scriptures! This only highlighted the fact, however, that they normally looked to local elders and deacons for leadership in studying the Scriptures and in maintaining their witness. I certainly saw enough, everywhere I went, to thank God for local leaders who against great odds were faithfully "flying the flag".

Mighty Men of Valour

It was, however, that unique handful of men endowed by God with the greatest gifts who carried the heaviest responsibilities. They had been raised up by Him, I am sure, in order to build up the churches and prepare them to face the fiery trials ahead. Many preachers are both gifted in preaching and upright in conduct. But the men I have in mind went a second mile. The "remuneration" to be expected for their gifted ministry was not material comfort and affluence but rather hardship and suffering — and eventually peril. But these considerations did not move them. Times of doubt and weakness there may have been, but they never turned back.

The exceptional ministry of these outstanding men was one of the earliest discoveries I made when with a fellow-recruit, Theodore Fischbacher, I left language school and began life in the northern province of Shanxi. We soon learned from our seniors that the churches in China owed a tremendous debt to three or four remarkable preachers whose influence was gradually spreading throughout the whole country.

Included in this book are some of the messages of a few of these outstanding men. The story of the indefatigable evangelist Dr John Sung is told in the biography of Leslie Lyall. Mr Wang Mingdao, who ministered in Peking, also edited a periodical entitled *The Spiritual Food Quarterly* which in due time was to be a great spiritual help to me. Some of Mr Wang's autobiographical writings appear in English in *A Stone Made Smooth* and other messages in *Spiritual Food* (Mayflower Christian Books, UK). The writings of Watchman Nee, whom I never met, are already widely circulated.

Not so well known are Pastor David Yang, who was to be our colleague in Shanxi, and the Rev. Chen Chonggui (Marcus Cheng) whom I knew more than ten years later when he was Principal of the Chongqing Theological Seminary.

The influence of all these men was immeasurably

extended through their writings, and it is this ministry that lies behind this present collection of translations.

I am thankful that the voices of these Chinese servants of God can now be heard more widely outside China. In reading or rereading the messages that were delivered so powerfully and influentially some 25 to 50 years ago I have been struck by their present-day relevance. The fact that the messages apply so widely, both geographically and chronologically, is undoubtedly because they are based on and permeated by the Word of God.

Acknowledgements

It was when my wife and I had to leave China in 1951 that we brought out the originals of most of the translations used in this book. However, I have also made use of some Chinese originals reprinted by Christian Literature Crusade in Hong Kong. They include the two messages by Dr John Sung and two (*They Hear — But Do They Heed? and The Royal Bride of Christ*) by Mr Wang Mingdao. We greatly appreciate the use of these reprints.

The translation of David Yang's message on *Perfected Saints* originally printed in *China's Millions*, was made by the late Miss Elizabeth Fischbacher. Miss Fishbacher was closely associated with the ministry of Pastor David Yang in the province of Shanxi.

Of course, none of these leaders is here set up as being free from shortcomings? Mr and Mrs Wang indicate that the process of smoothing the stone continues. And there is surely an element of Peter, with his startling inconsistencies, in all of us. In point of fact the examples set by these men are the more valuable in that although greatly used by God they are in the same waveband of potential weakness as ourselves. As the apostle Paul wrote to the Corinthians, "If you think you are standing firm, be careful that you don't fall!"

Men Who Made Their Mark

It remains true, however, that these men are mighty men of valour, men who made their mark. "We want again," said Charles Spurgeon, "Luthers, Calvins, Bunyans, Whitefields men fit to mark eras.... We have dire need of such. Whence will they come to us? They are the gifts of Jesus Christ to the Church, and will come in due time."[1]

Note that phrase of Spurgeon "Men fit to mark eras." Should we not now, in our own era, take up the cry of Spurgeon? For are we not in dire need of the John Sungs and the David Yangs and also — perhaps most of all — the Wang Mingdao's?

What is it that makes these men outstanding? What qualities have made them makers of history? In my view it is the combination of three notable features. Their gifts and abilities; their character and conduct; and their readiness to endure hardship. In other words, they have exercised a powerful and influential ministry of preaching; they have lived lives of known integrity; and as a consequence of their loyalty, both to the Lord and to the Faith, they have experienced hardship, loss, and persecution. They have been refined in the fire. These men are truly "the gifts of Jesus Christ to the Church".

Meanwhile, what all this means to us now is that the messages of these ministers are messages that carry authority.

1 Quoted in *The Narrow Way* (Cambridge) from *The Early Years* (Banner of Truth)

1 UNFOLDING THE GOSPEL

By grace you have been saved, through faith

Marcus Cheng (Chen Chonggui)

"IT IS BY GRACE you have been saved, through faith — and this not from yourselves, it is the gift of God." (Eph. 2:8)

1. Man's Need

Consider for a moment some of the emergencies that occur in human life. For example, someone falls into the water and when he is about to sink he calls out loudly, "Save me!" The situation is urgent. There was a similar cry for help when the disciples of the Lord Jesus were crossing the sea in a boat. They encountered a strong wind and huge waves met them, and the boat was about to sink. Fortunately the Lord Jesus was with them, but He was asleep. The disciples became alarmed and cried out in fear, "Lord! save us, we perish!" There is also the situation when someone is arrested for committing a capital offence. He will have to stand trial and in the normal way — if found guilty — would have to be punished. Obviously if he is to be pardoned something will have to be done quickly. An emergency also arises when someone swallows poison. If he is to be saved then treatment must be applied without delay.

These three situations may be regarded as symbolic of our spiritual situation. Our lives may be compared to travelling in a boat when we are constantly buffetted by storms. Think of all that we face in China. Inside the country there are calamities and disasters while from outside come other misfortunes. We sow the seeds of sin and we reap suffering and grief and trouble and death. Every day we read in the newspaper of people committing suicide. There are also people who are in fact committing suicide slowly — by indulging in gambling and licentiousness and so on. They are in urgent need of salvation. Within all of us is sin that operates like poison. Unless something is done it will destroy us. Who will save us?

2. God's Provision

There are two possible ways in which God can deal with us. He can deal with us according to law and punish us in accordance with our deserts or, since He is a God of love and compassion, He can treat us with grace.

God is God. His attributes are justice and holiness; they are also benevolence and compassion. In His dealings with men God cannot act contrary to His nature. He has indeed a wonderful way of saving men. It is set out for us in John 3:16 "For God so loved the world that He gave his one and only Son, that whoever believes in Him shall not perish but have eternal life." "God made him who had no sin to be sin for us, so that in him we might become the righteousness of God" (2 Cor. 5:21). He (Jesus) "was pierced for our transgression, he was crushed for our iniquities; the punishment that brought us peace was upon him, and by his wounds we are healed" (Isa. 53:5). Further, "we all, like sheep, have gone astray, each of us has turned to his own way; and the Lord has laid on him the iniquity of us all" (Isa. 53:6).

The apostle Paul wrote "It is by grace you have been saved." By grace. This is God's plan for sinners. Because our Saviour, the Lord Jesus, has borne the punishment for our sin, God does not further punish us according to the demands of justice. He deals with us in love and mercy — by grace. On our side it is "through faith". And the apostle adds, "and this not from yourselves, it is the gift of God — not by works, so that no-one can boast" (Eph. 2:8,9). There is another passage in the Bible in which the meaning of grace is exemplified. "When the kindness and love of God our Saviour appeared, he saved us, not because of righteous things that we had done, but because of his mercy." (Titus 2:4,5).

The door of grace is always open, and sinners are always free to enter. "Whoever comes to me," said Jesus, "I will never drive away" (John 6:37). When the prodigal son returned home the father received him with grace. But when the older brother saw how favourably the father was treating the younger son he was very angry. What did the father do then? He came outside and spoke kindly to the elder son. Our God is like that — a God of grace.

3. Man's Attitude
God for His part treats us with grace. But if we want

to be saved we must believe. Salvation is connected with faith no less than 150 times in the Bible. What do we mean by "faith"?

(a) Faith means believing that the words spoken by God are true. The prophets and apostles proclaim the words and commands of God, and we ought to obey them. Jesus is the Word of God, the incarnate Word. We ought to believe Him. The Lord Jesus said, "Come to me, all you who are weary and burdened, and I will give you rest" (Matt. 11:28). Do you or do you not believe that? If you believe it then you must come to Him.

(b) To believe in someone means to put one's trust in or to commit oneself to him. Men are saved because they put their trust in the Lord Jesus; they entrust themselves to Him. Just as when you board a ship you commit yourself wholly to the ship, so a sinner commits himself to the Saviour in order that his sins may be forgiven and he may be saved. Some people try to save themselves. They become vegetarians; they recite Scripture; they discipline themselves. It is like making one's own ladder to climb to heaven. But this is impossible. In America they have buildings of fifty storeys and in order to reach the top storey from the bottom it is only necessary to enter a lift and you are taken to the top. This is an illustration of the way of salvation. Our part is to entrust ourselves to the Saviour.

I emphasize that when we believe we must submit ourselves completely to the Lord. When we take medicine we speak of "submitting to medicine" and when we believe in the Lord Jesus it is to Him we submit. Faith is manifested in submission.

So if you are not already saved I urge you to put your trust in the Lord Jesus without delay.

The Salvation of Zaccheus

John Sung (Song Shangjie)

AT THIS FIRST meeting in our convention (at Amoy) I want to preach on a very precious passage of Scripture — Luke 19:1-10.

It was at Jericho that an important historical event entered Jericho a harlot, Rahab, concealed two spies from their pursuers. Afterwards all in the city except this family were destroyed, but because of Rahab's faith her whole family were saved. Anyone who entered Jericho after that would recall the interesting story of how God delivered Rahab and her family.

This occasion was the last time that Jesus entered Jericho. The Bible specifically mentions that He "was passing through". What a rare opportunity — unprecedented and not to be repeated!

Nowadays when merchants come to Amoy they want to walk down the wide streets along which the big stores are built. When students come to Amoy they want to look round the university. When a person who likes cinema-going comes he would obviously enquire for the cinemas. But when Jesus came to Jericho it was not to survey the scenery, nor was it to participate in the bustle and excitement. When He came to Jericho it was to save sinners.

Jesus has come to us here tonight for the same purpose. If you are a sinner still unsaved, it is you that Jesus has come to seek, and His objective is to save you. This is a very rare opportunity. It is an opportunity that for years has eluded you. I urge you to make the most of your opportunity this evening.

What kind of people were they to whom Jesus

went in Jericho? He went to seek those who in His eyes were of inestimable value — that is, sinners. We read in verse 2 that "a man was there by the name of Zaccheus." Zaccheus's name means "pure", but I fear that his name did not accord with reality.

Some of you who are sitting here this evening may have names such as "Heavenly Virtue", "Excellent Virtue", and so on, but I fear that those names do not accord with reality. Although the name Zaccheus meant "pure", he was a *lao-ban* (literally, a proprietor, but in North China a term of disrespect suggesting deviousness). He had sinned in many ways and become rich. But even a rich man can be saved. Jesus once said, "It is easier for a camel to go through the eye of a needle than for a rich man to enter the kingdom of God." (Matt. 19:24) But He added, "With man this is impossible, but with God all things are possible." (Matt. 19:26) So even a rich man can be saved. Even the name Zaccheus can be written in heaven.

What did Zaccheus possess? He had wealth; he had reputation; and he had authority. In fact he had virtually everything. But what he did not have was peace. Although he was a Jew it was through helping Rome that he had amassed his possessions. He was a traitor, and all the Jews hated him.

But it was just because he was so hated by men that he resolved to find Jesus and thus receive comfort.

It tells us in verse 3 that a great crowd followed Jesus. No matter where Jesus went there was always a crowd of people following him. Zaccheus was no exception; he too wanted to see Jesus. Perhaps he thought that Jesus could give him peace. Perhaps he had visited temples and called out to idols "Idols! Save me!" But no peace was forthcoming in that quarter. Now he went out to see Jesus — not to see men but to see Jesus. This is a lesson for us. Looking to men will not avail. It is Jesus whom we must seek.

Zaccheus was a rich man but he was not a tall man. He wanted to see Jesus but he was unable to do so. Beloved brothers and sisters! Outside the bounds of the church there are many people who want to see Jesus, but they are unable to see Him. Their hearts are set on gain and fame, thus making themselves figuratively short and fat. So Jesus is hidden from them.

But Zaccheus had made up his mind that come what may, he would not rest satisfied without seeing Jeus. He was able to find a sycamore tree which he climbed. Everybody would laugh at this man who was short and fat, but he took no notice of their laughter. He set on one side all thought of his social position. One thing only occupied his mind: he was a sinner and he wanted to see Jesus.

In many places I have visited officials have not dared to come publicly to listen to the gospel. One of them wrote to me, "Dr Sung! Please come to my home and have a meal with me. I want to hear you preach!" But in the case of Zaccheus it was different. He humbled himself and came openly, even climbing a tree, in order to see Jesus.

"When Jesus reached the spot, he looked up and said to him, 'Zaccheus, come down immediately. I must stay at your house today,'" (verse 5). These few words are enough to show the love and compassion of Jesus. Step by step he came to the spot where Zaccheus was, even right under the sycamore tree! Zaccheus must have thought that Jesus had made a mistake and taken the wrong road. Was that what had happened? Indeed it was not. Jesus had come expressly to find him. When Jesus reached the place under the tree He looked up at Zaccheus with a face that showed His love and compassion. Although in the middle of a crowd, Jesus did not look at the others, only at Zaccheus. For he had come expressly to seek and to save what was lost.

Then Jesus, lifting up His eyes, called out "Zaccheus! Zaccheus!" Jesus already knew his name. Never before had Zaccheus known anyone look at him in such a loving and compassionate manner, or address him in such a loving and compassionate tone of voice.

Jesus called out "Come down immediately!" And He added, "I must stay at your house today." Today! Salvation is today! You need not wait. Salvation is not for tomorrow or the day after tomorrow. It is for today. Jesus also said, "I must." Salvation is assured. There is nothing vague or uncertain about it. It is not a case of "near enough". So long as you are willing to accept the Lord you will be saved.

Beloved brothers and sisters! Our hearts are unclean like the home of Zaccheus, but Jesus is willing to come into our hearts. All we need to do is to let Him come in. One day I was in a certain place preaching the gospel, when a blind woman said to me, "Dr Sung! Although I am sightless I still fall into sin. I once sinned with another person and an illegitimate child was born. I then did away with the child. Is Jesus willing to save a person like me?"

I said, "Listen! Even though your heart is full of uncleaness, the blood of the Lord is enough to cleanse you. All you need do is to repent. Then the Holy Spirit will take up His abode in your heart."

In another place there were two sisters whose condition was extremely pitiable. In the province of Jiangxi their whole family had encountered bandits and had fled to Nanchang, where they were in dire straits because of their poverty. They could not bear to see their mother hungry and their brother starving, so they became prostitutes. The older sister reached the point where she could endure the life no more, and she had a nervous breakdown. Afterwards an army officer took pity on her and paid for her to be trained as a nurse. It was then that she heard me preaching and was moved by the message. "Dr Sung!" she asked, "Is the Lord willing to save a person like me?" "If you are willing to repent," I replied, "Jesus is willing to save even those who are worthy of death."

"Come down!" This symbolizes the fact that the first step in being saved is to humble oneself. It is not just a case of believing in the head or in the mouth; it is a matter of receiving the salvation of the Lord in your heart.

"So he came down at once and welcomed him gladly," (verse 6).

He did not delay, or decide to wait until he was approaching death — as some do — and then repent of his sin. He came down at once and welcomed Jesus.

All the people saw Jesus making His way to the home of Zaccheus, and then pandemonium broke out. They murmured, "Zaccheus is a sinner. Why does Jesus visit him in his home?" There were many other homes in Jericho, but Jesus did not choose to go to any of them. He went only to the home of Zaccheus. The people did not understand. There are many people today who do not really know Jesus and what He came for — that He came in order to save sinners.

Zaccheus called Jesus "Lord!" (verse 8). He discerned that Jesus was not merely a man; He was

Lord. Did Jesus put pressure on him to confess his sin? No! In the presence of Jesus he announced what he would do. "Lord! Here and now I give half of my possessions to the poor." Suppose he had 10,000 yuan, he would use 5,000 yuan to relieve people in need. That was not at all easy. But what he gave up was nothing compared with what he gained. He now had the Lord Jesus.

Zaccheus also promised, "If I have cheated anybody out of anything, I will pay back four times the amount." Ah! Restoring four-fold is not easy either. He felt unworthy to receive the Lord in his home. But he determined to repent. It was not a superficial or a merely nominal repentance, it was genuine and thoroughgoing. What about *your* repentance? Is it genuine?

Zaccheus was saved within a few minutes of hearing the voice of the Lord. On the tree he was an avaricious official; but under the tree he was a disciple of the Lord.

"Jesus said to him, 'Today salvation has come to this house, because this man, too, is a son of Abraham'" (verse 9). It was not a case of waiting. Even before Jesus reached the home of Zaccheus, salvation had already been accomplished. Jesus wanted to save not only Zaccheus but the whole family also.

Zaccheus was completely transformed within five minutes. By contrast there are many people today who have been in the church for many years and who are still not saved. Isn't that something to be lamented?

"For the Son of Man came to seek and to save what was lost" (verse 10).

It was as if Jesus said, "Zaccheus! I have come to save you. During these thirty years of my life I have suffered greatly and I shall eventually die on the cross. But Zaccheus! This is all for you. This is all to save *you*."

Beloved brothers and sisters! I would like to share with you my own experience and bear my testimony to the Lord. My father was a pastor and the whole family believed in the Lord. Not long after I was born I was baptized as an infant. I used to spend time in prayer and I used to read my Bible. But I did not really pray in my heart and I did not accept the Scriptures in my heart.

At the age of nineteen I went to study in America and as soon as I was engaged in acquiring an education I forgot the Lord. I came to look upon myself as possessing both learning and ability. Everything came to my hand, but one thing I did not find was peace. In fact on many occasions I was tempted to seek death. Other people saw me as having acquired an education and as being very happy. But they were quite unaware of my inner pain.

At first I looked upon Jesus as simply a good man and not as a Saviour. But praise the Lord! On the evening of February 10th, 1927, Jesus sought me — as He had once sought Zaccheus — there in America. Jesus came to Room No 415 at an atheistic theological college and there He found me. That evening the light of the Holy Spirit illumined me. I wept over my sin, for had I not wept the experience would have been even more bitter. I saw a light, and in that light Jesus said to me, "Child! I died for your sin." As a result of that experience I was completely changed.

Dear friends! It is my deep desire that the Lord Jesus who saved me that evening in America will also save you here today. Jesus forsook all the glories of heaven and came into the world for you and me. Although our sins may be deeper than the seas and higher than the mountains, the Lord Jesus can save every one of us. I pray that all of us may be saved this evening through the precious blood of the Lord Jesus.

2 <u>EXALTING</u>
<u>THE LORD</u>
JESUS CHRIST

Paul and the Scriptures

Marcus Cheng

"I DID NOT consult any man, nor did I go up to Jerusalem to see those who were apostles before I was, but I went immediately into Arabia and later returned to Damascus." (Gal. 1:16b,17)

We read of the Lord Jesus that after His baptism "he saw the Spirit of God descending like a dove and lighting on him. And a voice from heaven said, 'This is my Son, whom I love; with him I am well pleased,'" (Matt. 3:16,17). Immediately afterwards Jesus was led by the Spirit into the desert.

The apostle Paul had a similar experience. His eyes had been opened to see the Lord Jesus and he heard a voice from heaven. Immediately afterwards he departed for the desert of Arabia and there, in that secluded place, he was alone with God. Where was this place situated? In all probability it was Mount Sinai, the place where God had handed to Moses the stone tablets of the Testimony. There in Arabia Paul spent three years — or parts of three years — in prayer and meditation.

When Paul went to Arabia he had the five Books of Moses, the Psalms of David, and the Book of Isaiah. When he returned he also carried with him, in his heart and on his lips, the Book of Romans, the contents of the letters to the Ephesians, the Galatians, the Thessalonians, and so on. Most theological colleges and Bible colleges today provide a three-year study course for Christian workers. I pray that we may all learn lessons from the three years that Paul spent in Arabia.

At the beginning of his letter to the Galatians Paul made it clear that he was an apostle "sent not from men nor by man, but by Jesus Christ and God the Father, who raised him from the dead." It was a case of God taking the initiative in revealing His Son in the heart of Paul.

Paul read his Bible section by section and verse by verse and all of them pointed to Jesus. He opened his Bible at Genesis 1:1 and he read that "In the beginning God created the heavens and the earth." He then wrote "For by him (Jesus) all things were created: things in heaven and on earth, visible and invisible, whether thrones or powers or rulers or authorities; all things were created by him and for him" (Col. 1:16).

Paul read in Genesis that "God said, 'Let there be light,' and there was light" (1:3). He then wrote, "For God, who said, 'Let light shine out of darkness,' made his light shine in our hearts to give us the light of knowledge of the glory of God in the face of Christ" (2 Cor. 4:6).

When the Lord God made a woman from the rib he had taken out of Adam, Adam said, "This is now bone of my bones and flesh of my flesh; she shall be called 'woman', for she was taken out of man" (Gen.

2:23). Paul wrote, with reference to this, "This is a profound mystery — but I am talking about Christ and the church" (Eph. 5:32).

Paul's lips and Paul's heart were alike full of Jesus. He perceived clearly that the Bible had only one theme — and that theme was Jesus. So Paul's preaching and writing had only one theme also. It was Jesus.

Mary Breaks An Alabaster Jar
(Mark 14:3-9)

John Sung

CONSIDER the situation recorded in this passage. Jesus was at Bethany in the home of a man known as Simon the leper, whose leprosy had been cured by the Lord. He felt overwhelmingly grateful to the Lord, and as an expression of his gratitude he prepared a feast and invited the Lord Jesus to attend. It was during the feast that a woman came with an alabaster jar of very expensive perfume. The Gospel of John tells us that this was Mary, the younger sister of Lazarus. Once Jesus had visited their home when the sisters were busy waiting on Jesus. So they were not sufficiently well-off to hire a helper. Then their brother Lazarus had died and the Lord had raised him from the dead. This had brought Mary great joy and she could not restrain herself from expressing her gratitude. Hearing that the Lord Jesus was in the home of Simon she joyfully made her way there bringing an alabaster jar of perfume.

During the years that the Lord Jesus was on earth a large number of events took place. Among them there were only two that we are especially told to remember. First, we are to remember the Lord's Table. And second, we are to remember the action of the woman in the home of Simon the leper. The Bible tells us of many famous women, yet we are not called on to remember any of them in a special way. But the Lord does call on us to remember this particular woman. Why? It was because she brought an alabaster jar which contained a most expensive perfume of pure nard, fragrant and beautiful, which she used to anoint the Lord.

It was not a synthetic perfume; it was genuine. And it was extremely valuable.

Beloved brothers and sisters! When we read the Scriptures we need to pay attention to every word. Take note of the words here — alabaster jar, very expensive, pure (i.e. genuine) nard, perfume. If we were the ones performing this act we should probably pour out the perfume from the container without breaking it. But this woman broke the jar so that it filled her hands. She then anointed Jesus. It signified that she loved the Lord with an undivided devotion. Nothing was too expensive to hold back. She did not regard the breaking of the alabaster jar as loss. Although she came from a poor home the spending of more than 300 denarii (more than a year's wages) did not figure in her reckoning.

This woman greatly loved the Lord Jesus. She not only exercised faith, she also performed deeds. We may regard the alabaster jar as representing our physical being while the perfume may be seen as representing love. We must present ourselves to the Lord wholly — our bodies and our souls. And we must be prepared to sacrifice all.

Many parents make sacrifices for their children. There are wives who make sacrifices for their husbands. A certain woman I have in mind worked so hard for her husband over a period of eight years that she developed tuberculosis. What she did was to sacrifice her own precious self — the alabaster jar — for her husband. There are other people who break the alabaster jar in working hard for a living. In the case of this woman what she did was for Jesus. It was for Him that she made the sacrifice.

I sometimes wonder whether there is anyone in the whole world who really loves Jesus in this way. Judas was one whom Jesus loved, but Judas betrayed Him. When Jesus was arrested his disciples scattered through fear of death. Beloved brothers and sisters! The Lord Jesus once said, "Foxes have holes and birds of the air have nests, but the Son of Man has no place to lay his head" (Luke 9:58). Once as Jesus travelled in the company of his disciples, he became hungry. At that point He came across a fig tree at the roadside with an abundance of foliage. The Lord went up to it and inspected it, but no fruit did He find.

Even though you search the whole world, where will you find people who wholly love the Lord like this woman did? The Lord Jesus healed people with all kinds of diseases; He drove out demons; He had compassion on the people gathered in the wilderness and with five loaves and two fishes He fed the multitude. Even so, we look in vain for those who wholly love the Lord. Yet shortly before He was to depart from the world a woman showed that she truly loved Him. This was certainly not an easy thing to do. The Bible tells us that it was "very expensive perfume of pure nard." It was genuine. Because this woman loved Jesus she broke the alabaster jar and the room was filled with the fragrance. It was to glorify the Lord.

The loss of the alabaster jar was trivial in the light of the Lord's preciousness. Her money was expendable; her body was expendable; her life was expendable. It was only the Lord who counted; it was only He who was precious. There were those who tried to stop her, but she went through with it.

Several people present displayed their displeasure. It is to be feared that some of the disciples — Peter, John, James, Andrew — were also displeased. They were in the mood to complain, "Why this waste of perfume?" Bystanders who basically had no love for Jesus were also involved. Although they did not clearly speak out, they murmured against her.

Was this sister really wasting the perfume? Of course not! The Lord sees men's hearts; He is not swayed by external appearances. Jesus listened carefully and then revealed His evaluation. "She has done a beautiful thing for me." Brothers and sisters! Don't let us forget! It is true now as it was then that the Lord Jesus can see into our hearts. It was not merely a case of their not being joyful; they were very angry. All that this woman did was to show her love for the Lord, and yet the disciples were angry. They not only refrained from encouraging her, they went to the extent of pouring cold water over her enthusiasm.

Many people today speak as if the most important thing in life is to serve society, and we are swayed this way and that way, but all to no avail. In meetings for young people; in meetings to promote this or that; in annual meetings and so on the faction characterized by liberal theology seems to regard good deeds as of more importance than showing one's love for the Lord Jesus. In their eyes to magnify the Lord Jesus is wasteful and not worthwhile.

I am often pitied for wearing out my physical frame in preaching. A certain highly-placed executive once said to me, "Dr Sung! You are much to be pitied. You are wasting your time. Why is it that someone with your ability is not spending his time in serving society? Why are you not doing something for people in general? Why is it that all you do revolves around Jesus?"

Judas was among those who thought it was a good thing to serve society. He coveted thirty pieces of silver and he sold Jesus for thirty pieces of silver. Many people who serve society are really serving themselves, and the Lord looks upon people like that as thieves. It is only by your willingness to make sacrifices for Jesus that you can show your love for Jesus. Otherwise you cannot be reckoned as truly loving Him. Many liberals are engaged in promoting social movements and social service. Their preaching amounts to a good deal of beating of drums, but the name of Jesus is never mentioned. Even less is any reference made to redemption through Jesus' blood.

Somebody said to me, "Dr Sung! Why do you say so much and why do you sing so much about Jesus?" I tell you. This woman showed her love for Jesus and the people around her gave her black looks. Our Lord was in the world for 33 years and how many people really showed their love for Him? Even His own disciples have to be counted out. And in our day, how many people really and wholly love Jesus? Yet this woman did. She loved the Lord and for His sake she broke an alabaster jar of perfume. She wanted to show her gratitude for the grace that the Lord had bestowed upon her, and yet she had nothing with which to recompense Him. All she could do was to sacrifice herself. In that way she sought to bring Him glory.

It was indeed a beautiful thing that she did. And it brought great joy to the Lord. Even angels were pleased. There are so few people on earth who really love the Lord, but here was a woman who did!

Judas! Leave her alone! Why hinder her? It is the petty people today, I fear, who are bent on hindering the work. Is Mary disheartened? Indeed she is not. Brothers and sisters! Don't be afraid! Just carry on! Bend every effort and carry on!

Jesus went on to say, "The poor you will always have with you, and you can help them any time you want. But you will not always have me," (verse 7). It is not that He disapproves of relieving the poor. It is simply that this kind of service may be rendered at any time and in any place.

What is the special significance of what this woman did? The Lord commented that it was to prepare for His burial. How many people thought about His burial? The disciples who had been with the Lord for three years certainly did not. It was this sister whom God used to administer comfort to Jesus.

My beloved brothers and sisters! The Lord has done great things for us. In redeeming us with His precious blood He himself broke an alabaster jar and by so doing released the fragrance of His love. And what He did was all on our account. How shall we show our gratitude for what the Lord did for us? What the woman did was to break the alabaster jar of perfume. In that way she showed her love. In what way shall we show that we too love the Lord?

No matter where the gospel is preached — whether in Amoy, or throughout China or anywhere under heaven — in all those places will this woman be remembered. There is no record of Jesus calling on His followers to tell of Mary, or the apostle John, or the old prophets, or the high priests, or famous kings. It is true of course that many people especially remember Peter, or James, but when Jesus said "wherever the gospel is preached throughout the world, what she has done will also be told, in memory of her", He was speaking of this particular woman.

The fragrance of what this woman did has persisted all down the years until the present. Of all the events that have occurred throughout the world all through the centuries the vast majority are not worth remembering. Yet wherever the gospel is preached we shall remember this woman. The Lord Himself remembered it; you also remember it; and so will those in every place where the gospel is preached. Whenever someone important dies people immediately get busy arranging memorial services and putting up memorial stones. But all these are man-made and the effect does not last indefinitely. Jesus never called on His followers to remember those who simply serve society. What they do can never be compared with what this woman did.

Jesus gave His life for us. In what way, apart from bearing His cross, can we bring Him comfort? In the end our bodies will disintegrate and our voices be silenced. It is true that people can use gramophone records to preserve people's voices and thus remember them. Our features will inevitably bear the marks of age, so people take photographs to preserve our appearance when young. But if we are to be remembered in a way that endures there is only one way to do it. We must for the Lord's sake break the alabaster jar. And we must offer ourselves entirely to God. One day, inevitably, you will pass on from this world and the memorial stones that are set up may indeed be designed to carry fragrant memories for a hundred generations. Do not be deluded into thinking that even this can be guaranteed. The fragrance of Mary's alabaster jar has survived until the present. But the home of Simon is no more and all that belonged to Judas has been obliterated. All the perfume in the alabaster jar was poured out and the fragrance has endured. It still remains.

The time will come, and perhaps soon, when you must pass on. What will you do now for the Lord? The Lord broke the alabaster jar — in other words He shed His blood and died for our redemption. He did all that for us. What, then, shall we do for Him?

3   LAYING FOUNDATIONS

What are the essential features of the Gospel?

Marcus Cheng

IF YOU were to ask the apostle Paul, "What is of importance in the gospel?", he would undoubtedly reply, "Brothers...what I received I passed on to you as of first importance: that Christ died for our sins according to the Scriptures, that he was buried, that he was raised on the third day according to the Scriptures, and that he appeared to Peter..." (1 Cor. 15:1-4).

Suppose you went on to address the apostle as follows: "When you in your day preached the gospel you naturally centred your teaching in Jesus crucified and risen from the dead. But circumstances in China at the present time are so vastly different from those of your day, so may we not change the emphasis and preach — for example — various 'isms'? Can we not preach the culture and philosophy of the West?"

At this point I must interject a warning. If you presume to ask the apostle questions like this you must be prepared for an uncompromising reply. For he has already answered such questions. This is what he wrote to the Galatians. "I am astonished that you are so quickly deserting the one who called you by the grace of Christ and are turning to a different gospel — which is really no gospel at all. Evidently some people are throwing you into confusion and are trying to pervert the gospel of Christ. But even if we or an angel from heaven should preach a gospel other than the one we preached to you, let him be eternally condemned! As we have already said, so now I say again. If anybody is preaching to you a gospel other than what you accepted, let him be eternally condemned!" (Gal.1:6-9)

No one can read the Book of Acts and the letters of the apostles and legitimately refuse to acknowledge that, when the apostles preached the gospel, the essential doctrines they stressed were related to Jesus crucified and raised from the dead. The life of the apostles, the faith of the apostles, the work of the apostles — all these things were built on that one firm foundation.

That is why the apostle Paul wrote, "If Christ has not been raised, our preaching is useless and so is your faith" (1 Cor. 15:14).

So let us give thanks to God. For Christ has indeed been raised from the dead. This is both the ground and the guarantee of this marvellous fact — that neither our preaching nor our faith can ever be discarded as useless.

The Relevance of the Atonement

Wang Mingdao

NOT LONG AGO I was invited by a Christian brother to have a meal with him in Shanghai. After we had eaten our meal we read from a book in which there was an account of a convicted murderer who had heard the gospel and been converted while in prison. In his diary there were passages that made you rejoice and others that made you weep. His character had been completely reformed and his subsequent experiences amply demonstrated the power of Christ and the wonder of salvation. But at the close of the book it was announced that, being convicted of a capital offence, he had eventually been executed. The reader was shown a photograph of the grave.

Having finished our meal we discussed together this man's circumstances. We concluded unanimously that since he had repented and reformed, the court ought to have exercised mercy and given him a pardon. Even if a full pardon was hardly feasible we still felt that the court should have acted leniently and thought up some other form of punishment. How could even a court of law be so unfeeling as to refuse to exercise any mercy in their treatment of a criminal who had demonstrated his contrition and repentance?

As we talked about this matter I sat on my chair deep in thought. It seemed truly strange. Was not God's law even more severe than man's law? Was not God holier than men? And did not God hate sin more than man did? If that was so, was it not perplexing that one who had repented of his sin could be forgiven by God but not forgiven by man?

Did this not show that men were malicious and cruel and vindictive?

I continued to ponder this question when suddenly an important truth lit up my heart like a flash of lightning. It was not anything new. I had in fact proclaimed this truth for more than ten years. But there came to me a greater understanding of it than I had ever known before. The explanation was clear. God could forgive this man, greatly though he had sinned, because where God was concerned there was a Saviour. That Saviour had already accepted punishment and died in his place. Yet where the laws of the land were concerned there was no arrangement (and indeed there could not be) for a saviour to die in his place. So although he had shown contrition and had repented, it was still necessary for him to undergo the punishment ordained by the law.

Since we ourselves had been moved by love and compassion towards a man who had repented, we failed to understand how the judge in that case could not show compassion also. The fact is, the law demanded death for a murderer. So even though the judge himself was moved by compassion more than any man, there was nothing he could do about it. He was only carrying out his duty. He was in fact faithful in carrying out the law. Since the law required the death of such a criminal, the judge had no authority to act differently.

Do you see the point? The offended in this case had committed murder. He had broken both the law of God and the law of the land. As one who had broken the law of God he should expect to be punished by God, and since he had also broken the law of the land he should expect to be punished by the law of the land. The law of God cannot be changed; the law of the land cannot be changed. But where God is concerned there is a Saviour who has tasted death in the place of trangressors, so that when a transgressor repents he is forgiven by God and saved from the punishment that would otherwise be his due. But where the state is concerned no saviour is provided. So although the transgressor repents in deep contrition he cannot be forgiven or escape the punishment.

From all this it becomes apparent that a sinner stands in great need of a Saviour. A sinner, in order to be saved, must repent and confess his sin. But that by itself is not enough. Without the atoning sacrifice of Christ, no matter how thoroughly men repent and confess their sin, they still cannot escape punishment. It is not our repentance that saves us; it is the Lord. He died in order to save us. The law of the land cannot be changed; even less can the law of God be changed. So were there no Christ to die for our sin there would be no way of escaping the punishment ordained.

In view of this there is a tendency in the church today that is extremely saddening. Many preachers proclaim a message, and many seminary professors teach a theology, from which the atoning sacrifice of Christ is absent. These teachers and preachers may be divided into two categories. Some simply keep silent and never deal with the doctrine of the atonement at all; others not only publicly repudiate this doctrine but do not hesitate to denounce those who proclaim it. They assert that the doctrine of the atonement is merely a religious concept of the ancient Israelites, and they aver that the reason Paul had much to say on the subject was that he was a Jew whose mind had been deeply influenced by the doctrines passed on by the Jews. They even go so far as to say that Jesus Himself never preached this doctrine. That of course is totally incorrect, for Jesus proclaimed it repeatedly.

The fact is, most preachers and teachers who reject the doctrine of the atonement also reject other basic doctrines. They do not believe in promises about the future life; they do not accept the basic doctrine of the resurrection. This is not really strange. For without Christ's work of atonement there can be no salvation, no forgiveness of sin and no eternal life. Moreover, how can you fit in the promises about the future? And when these preachers dispense with the atonement they have to put other things in its place — improvement of character; the reformation of society; the service of the people; and so on.

Thank God! Christ has died in the place of sinners. "Surely he took up our infirmities and carried our sorrows, yet we considered him stricken by God, smitten by him, and afflicted. But he was pierced for our transgressions, he was crushed for our iniquities; the punishment that brought us peace was upon him, and by his wounds we are healed. We all, like sheep, have gone astray, each of us has turned to his own way; and the Lord has laid on him the iniquity of us all" (Isa. 53:4-6). "The Son of Man did not come to be served, but to serve, and to give his life as a ransom for many" (Matt. 20:28). "He himself bore our sins in his body on the tree, so that we might die to sins and live for righteousness; by his wounds you have been healed" (1 Pet. 2:24).

We thank God because Christ for our sakes not only died but also rose again. He broke the bonds of death. His resurrection tells us that His work of atonement has satisfied the heart of God. Because of His resurrection we know for certain that our trust in Him is not in vain, that He has smashed the power of death, and that we too will rise again. Jesus said,

"I am the resurrection and the life. He who believes in me will live, even though he dies, and whoever lives and believes in me will never die" (John 11:25). These words are utterly trustworthy; who can question them? He who died and rose again is our Saviour, our Mediator, and our Friend. How happy we ought to be!

In the light of all this we can appreciate all the more what the apostle Paul wrote to the Romans: "Who will bring any charge against those whom God has chosen? It is God who justifies. Who is he that condemns? Christ Jesus, who died — more than that, who was raised to life — is at the right hand of God and is also interceding for us" (Rom. 8:33,34).

Paul was the apostle whom the Lord Jesus Himself selected and sent forth. Let us go over again and again the words he wrote to the Corinthians: "Now, brothers, I want to remind you of the gospel I preached to you, which you received and on which you have taken your stand. By this gospel you are saved, if you hold firmly to the word I preached to you. Otherwise you have believed in vain. For what I received I passed on to you as of first importance, that Christ died for our sins according to the Scriptures, that he was buried, that he was raised on the third day according to the Scriptures" (1 Cor. 15:1-4).

It was in such a gospel that our salvation, our peace, our joy and our hope originated. May all of us who have been redeemed by the precious blood of Christ put our full trust in these basic truths. And let us strive in every possible way to spread this gospel!

Reconciliation

Marcus Cheng

"GOD, who reconciled us to himself through Christ..
...We implore you on Christ's behalf: Be reconciled
to God" (2 Cor. 5:18, 20).

On first reading these two verses one is struck by
what appears to be a rather curious circumstance. Is
it not man who needs to be reconciled to God? Is it a
fact that God takes the initiative and reconciles
Himself to man? And is man so unwilling to be
reconciled to God that it is necessary for God to call
on him to seek reconciliation? Strange as it may
seem, this is in fact the situation.

(At this point the writer discusses the two Chinese
ideographs that make up the Chinese word 'reconciliation'.)

Men in their relationship to God, are not keepers
of the law but rebels against it. Men are not filial and
obedient children but stubborn and undutiful prodigals. Men are not the friends of God but the
enemies of God. Because of their evil ways, and
because in their hearts they have become God's
enemies, men have been separated from God. When
we look around us we see abundant evidence of this,
and this general picture is a reflection of what we see
in our own hearts when we pause to examine
ourselves.

What is the gospel of the Lord Jesus Christ? It is
the good news of reconciliation between man and
God. Men are out of harmony with God, separated
from Him, hostile to Him; they are God's enemies.
But God took the initiative in reconciliation by
sending His only begotten Son into the world in

order to seek the lost. He came to reveal God as Father. God is love and will welcome returning prodigals. The Lord Jesus Christ shed His blood and laid down His life on the cross for mankind. This is in fact where we see God reconciling the world to Himself.

More than this, it is God's purpose that this doctrine of reconciliation should be proclaimed throughout the whole world. So He has ordained that those who are already reconciled to God should be His messengers, and that on His behalf they should urge men to be reconciled to Him.

1. Why do men need to be reconciled to God?

Because it is on reconciliation that their joy, peace and well-being depend! The universe and all its constituent parts are in harmony with God, and obedient to Him. Within the harmony of the universe it only requires that men be reconciled to God and all things will work together for good (Rom. 8:28). But otherwise, if men are not reconciled to God, then we may say that all things work together for harm.

In your home, if you are not in harmony with the head of the household, can you share the joy of that home? In your country, if you rebel against the government, can you share the peace of the country? In the whole world, if you are not in harmony with the Creator, can you expect to share its joy and peace and happiness?

The prophet Jeremiah wrote: "'Your wickedness will punish you; your backsliding will rebuke you. Consider then and realize how evil and bitter it is for you when you forsake the Lord your God and have no awe of me', declares the Lord, the Lord

Almighty" (Jer. 2:19).

Evil is itself punishment. Your wickedness will punish you. Countless men and women can testify to this truth from their own experiences. Should not a notice be put up outside the gateway of a prison — and outside the gateway of hell — "Your wickedness will punish you!"? It is perfectly clear from Jeremiah 2:19 that if we forsake the Lord our God and refrain from worshipping Him, and instead engage in wickedness, that is what adds up to bitterness. God said to man, "The fear of the Lord, that is wisdom, and to shun evil is understanding" (Job 28:28).

2. How can we be reconciled to God?

There are two sides to this process, God's side, and man's side. The initiative was taken by God. God enabled man to be reconciled to Him through the incarnation of Christ and particularly through His death. "God made him who had no sin to be sin for us, so that in him we might become the righteousness of God" (2 Cor. 5:21). God is righteous; man is unrighteous. A righteous God and unrighteous man cannot be reconciled. If there is to be a reconciliation it can only be achieved in one way — by making the unrighteous man to be righteous.

But how can unrighteous man become righteous before God? The answer: through Jesus Christ being crucified for men, shedding His blood and giving His life so that men may be justified and sanctified. Only in this way can unrighteous man and righteous God be reconciled. The Lord Jesus only accomplished the great work of reconciliation by paying a very heavy price and by making a very great sacrifice.

"Surely he took up our infirmities and carried our sorrows, yet we considered him stricken by God, smitten by him, and afflicted. But he was pierced for our transgressions, he was crushed for our iniquities; the punishment that brought us peace was upon him, and by his wounds we are healed. We all, like sheep, have gone astray, each of us has turned to his own way, and the Lord has laid on him the iniquity of us all" (Isa. 53:4-6).

God for His part has left nothing whatever undone in preparing the way for man to be reconciled to God. All that remains is for man to do his part.

Firstly, man needs to come into the presence of God and to be reconciled to Him. Like the prodigal described by the Lord Jesus man needs to come to himself, to arise and to return home into the presence of the father. The Lord said, "Come now, let us reason together...Though your sins are like scarlet, they shall be as white as snow; though they are red as crimson, they shall be like wool" (Isa. 1:18). And from the Lord comes the following declaration: "'Return, faithless Israel,' declares the Lord, 'I will frown on you no longer, for I am merciful,' declares the Lord, 'I will not be angry for ever. Only acknowledge your guilt — you have rebelled against the Lord your God, you have scattered your favours to foreign gods under every spreading tree, and have not obeyed me,' declares the Lord" (Jer. 3:22,12,13).

Secondly, men need to believe the words of God, and to receive God's grace, putting their trust in Jesus the Saviour. Thus they are given a new standing and become heir to Christ's new way of life.

So God's part is active while man's part is passive. God speaks; man believes. God bestows; man receives. So it is that man is reconciled to God.

3. When can man be reconciled to God?

The Bible answers this question very clearly. "I tell you, now is the time of God's favour, now is the day of salvation" (2 Cor. 6:2).

It is made plain in this verse that although God bestows His grace upon us, the period during which it is available to us is limited.

When the period ordained by God has been completed, the offer of His grace is no longer valid. But thanks be to God! This is still the time of God's favour; this is still the day of salvation. So if we would be reconciled to God, we must grasp our opportunity now.

It is not uncommon for Christian teaching to be seriously misunderstood. Some people regard religion as simply a preparation for life after death, and therefore meaningful only for older people. Naturally, the matter of reconciliation to God is indeed very relevant to the question of life after death. It has everything to do with our gaining entrance to heaven and being for ever with the Lord. Yet religion is also essential for our everyday life now, and in fact has special significance for young people whose life streches before them. It is vitally important that they be reconciled to God. If you are young and you want your whole life to be bright and happy, meaningful and strong, then you need to be reconciled to God without delay. For if you are reconciled to God you will be reconciled to man. On the other hand, if you are not right with God you will not be right with man either.

Think carefully! What kind of person are you? Can you dare to be at enmity with God? In the eyes of God are you not a rebel? If so, it is impossible for you to live a life of serenity. Therefore God says, "I take no pleasure in the death of the wicked, but rather that they turn from their ways and live" (Ezek. 33:11). Now is the time of God's favour; now is the day of salvation. "Turn! Turn from your evil ways! Why will you die?" (Ezek. 33:11)

An elderly gentleman heard the gospel when he was 65 years old, and thereupon repented. He was full of joy because in the eventide of life, when he was drawing near to the grave, he was reconciled to God and saved. This man had three sons and several grandchildren. He urged them all to attend worship services and to listen to teaching from the Bible. But he was unprepared for their response. The eldest son replied, "Father! I shall not reach the age of 65 for some time, so why should I believe in religion now?" The second son replied, "Father! Wait until I am 65 like you and I will then go to church." The third son replied, "Father! Wait until I am 65 and if I then repent it will not be too late." The grandchildren answered in the same strain. "We will follow grandfather's example and when we reach the age of 65 we will go to church and listen to the teaching from the Bible." On hearing the children and grandchildren answer like this the elderly gentleman was very sad. He wept as he lamented, "I would cut off my right hand if I could only recover the years that I have wasted, the years of lost influence. I am extremely thankful to God that I was saved in the sunset years of my life, but how can I recover the years I have lost?"

Are there among the readers of this message any older people? If you are not yet reconciled to God I urge you to grasp this opportunity and to turn to God without delay. And what about those who are young? I urge you to remember your Creator in the days of your youth. Turn to God in repentance, and be reconciled to Him, before the days come when your strength begins to leave you. With Proverbs 4:18 before me I can assure you that your life will then be "like the first gleam of dawn, shining ever brighter till the full light of day."

No one can snatch them out of my hand

Marcus Cheng

"I GIVE THEM eternal life, and they shall never perish; no one can snatch them out of my hand. My Father, who has given them to me, is greater than all, no one can snatch them out of my Father's hand" (John 10:28, 29).

The Lord Jesus twice made the statement that the believer would not be snatched away. First it was from the hand of the Son, and second it was from the hand of the Father.

What do we know of these hands? They are the hands that rule heaven and earth. God needed no more than His fingers to create heaven and earth. With the palm of His hand He could measure the waters of the ocean. With the space between little finger and thumb He could measure the heavens.

Jesus knew that the Father had already handed over all things into His hand. With hands like this — hands that hold us fast — who can pull us away? Ponder these wonderful words! Believing and obeying the word of grace you can rest at ease. Never forget these words of Jesus! None can snatch us away.

The Lord Jesus also said, "My sheep listen to my voice; I know them, and they follow me. I give them eternal life, and they shall never perish; no one can snatch them out of my hand" (verses 27, 28). Thanks be to God our Saviour. He not only saves us He keeps us. He has given us eternal life and we can never perish.

These words of Jesus can be viewed in two ways. First there is God's side, which we see in Jude 24: "To him who is able to keep you from falling and to present you before his glorious presence without fault and with great joy."

Then there is man's side. Read Jude 20, 21. "But you, dear friends, build yourselves up in your most holy faith and pray in the Holy Spirit. Keep yourselves in God's love as you wait for the mercy of our Lord Jesus Christ to bring you to eternal life."

Take note of these four exhortations:
(1) Build yourselves up in your most holy faith
(2) Pray in the Holy Spirit
(3) Keep yourselves in God's love
(4) Wait for the mercy of our Lord Jesus Christ.

Believers who follow this advice of Jude need never be afraid of stumbling.

4

BUILDING UP THE CHURCH

Saints, Christians, and Church Members

Wang Mingdao

THE WORD "SAINT" is a designation commonly used in the letters of the apostles to describe those who believe in the Lord. In the four gospels and in the Book of Acts the word mostly used is "disciple", yet in the apostolic letters and in the Book of Revelation the normal designation is "saint". It has the meaning of being separated to holiness. Through the blood that was shed by the Lord Jesus, all who repent and believe in Him are completely cleansed and made holy.

Among the people of Corinth there had been thieves, drunkards, slanderers and so on. So when the apostle Paul wrote to the Corinthian believers he reminded them of this. "And that is what some of you were. But you were washed, you were sanctified, you were justified in the name of the Lord Jesus Christ and by the Spirit of God" (1 Cor. 6:11). No matter how unclean and evil a sinner is, all he needs to do is to repent and truly to believe in Christ and he is then completely cleansed. He becomes holy; he is separated from the world and separated to God. In other words, he is a saint.

From the relevant passages of Scripture[1] we find that all who believe in the Lord Jesus are described as saints. They qualify for such a designation irrespective of whether they have believed in the Lord for a long time or for only a short time, whether their spiritual experience is shallow or profound. So long as a person truly believes in the Lord he is a saint.

Note what Paul wrote to the believers at Ephesus: "For this reason, ever since I heard about your faith in the Lord Jesus and your love for all the saints, I have not stopped giving thanks for you, remembering you in my prayers" (Eph. 1:16). In the light of these words it does not seem strange that he addressed his letter "to the saints in Ephesus". But we must remember that he also described the Corinthian believers as "sanctified in Christ Jesus". And those believers were characterized by envy and strife; they tolerated adulterers; and they went to law before unbelievers.

The basis of our being designated saints is not that we are particularly virtuous but because we are in Christ. Those who have long believed in the Lord are saints; and those who have only recently believed in the Lord are equally saints. Mature believers who can take strong meat are saints, and carnal believers who can take milk are equally saints. Believers who live lives of victory are saints and believers who live lives of defeat are equally saints.

Naturally there are differences among saints. There is a distinction between those with high standards and those with low standards, between those who are spiritual and those who are carnal. And there is a distinction in the degree of their

[1] see page 45

likeness to Christ. But there is no distinction in regard to their standing as saints.

Since the designation "saint" is used in the Bible so widely, one would think that no true believer would hesitate to adopt it for himself. However, only a few venture to use it. Some Christians regard it as so sacred and exalted that it should be applied only to believers like Peter, John, James, Paul, Silas, Barnabas, Timothy and other extremely devout believers of the past. This is why they refer to St Peter or St Paul. The word is also used of certain specially devout and zealous believers of other ages, such as St Augustine and St Francis. But if you go so far as to give this title to people now living, this will be regarded with amazement. And if you go even further and refer to yourself as a saint, you will be accused of being presumptuous, proud and boastful.

So there is an anomaly. The meaning and significance of the word "saint" are set out in the Bible without ambiguity, yet countless believers who daily read their Bibles still do not grasp its significance or make use of it. The reason is not far to seek. It is that while all believers have access to the teaching of the Bible, many are prone to be more influenced by tradition.

In view of the fact that the connotation of "saint" has been so radically changed, how do the churches commonly describe those who believe in the Lord? They are called "church members". Since believers do not presume to continue the term so widely used in the Bible they substitute a designation thought up by man. So what happens? The churches are filled with "male church members", "female church members", "new church members", "old church members", "young church members", and so on. Yet even though you search your Bible from Genesis to Revelation you will never come across such an expression.

On a par with this practice is that of describing people who have repented and turned to the Lord as "entering the teaching (or religion)". Such a phrase is neither donkey nor horse. For unbelievers to speak in this way would not strike us as strange, but when the practice is taken over by believers it then becomes mysterious and mystifying.

The fact is, we should not only base our doctrines on the Bible, but we should also base our expressions on the Bible. The reason we make this assertion is that all the designations used in the Bible have their appropriate meanings. Since God through His servants has provided us with terminology that is distinguished and impressive, why do we not make use of it?

There is in Scripture yet another designation, which has been employed both carelessly and excessively: the designation "Christian". It is often asserted that this designation was orginally bestowed on believers by non-believers, and that it was used as an expression of disparagement. But we must ask whether such an interpretation is justified.

We read in Acts 11:26 that "The disciples were first called Christians at Antioch." The expression "called Christians" may be interpreted as either "called themselves Christians" or "were called Christians by others". By whom were they called Christians? Are there any grounds for asserting that the disciples were first called Christians by unbelievers? In the original language the word translated "called" is *chrematizo*. This word is used altogether nine times in the New Testament, and in each case it indicates that God expressed Himself to man. (See Matt. 2:12,22; Luke 2:26; Acts 11:26; Rom. 7:3;

Heb. 8:5, 11:7 and 12:15.) In the Chinese Bible it is translated variously as "to signify" (four times), "to warn" (twice), "to reveal" (once), and "to call" (once). In each case it is concerned with something that is done by God. So, when we read that "the disciples were called Christians" we understand it as meaning that it was *God* who so designated them. The meaning of "Christian" is "belonging to Christ". It is not merely a nickname chosen by unbelievers but an honourable designation bestowed on them by God.

Unfortunately the word "Christian" is used far too loosely. It is often applied to people who are not really Christians, for example those who join a church in order to receive material or financial help, to please their employers or superiors, to make friends of people of the opposite sex, to gain prestige or respect, or to get help in educating their children. People in all these categories are called "Christians" irrespective of their spiritual experience.

Let us suppose that, at the present time, we could gather together all who are described as "Christians" and then make careful enquiries as to their faith and their manner of life. I fear that the number of true Christians would not reach 20% or 30%. So while the designation "saint" is used too narrowly the designation "Christian" is used too widely. And while the number of actual saints is far in excess of the number normally described as saints, the number of true Christians is far below the number normally described as Christians. The number of Christians is limited to those who are qualified to be called saints. On the other hand, all true Christians are saints.

Many churches, when receiving new members, are apt to make the mistake of accepting them without adequate enquiry as to whether they really have faith or spiritual life, and whether they really know Christ. Nor do the churches enquire about their manner of life. They merely enquire about the applicant's knowledge of the Bible and the faith, and on that basis they receive them. Other churches do not go even as far as this. They ask a few questions haphazardly and then go ahead and baptize them. From that time on the people baptized are regarded as Christians.

I was once an observer at the baptismal service of ten people. The pastor stood in front of the pulpit and the candidates for baptism stood in line facing him. He then read a statement of faith and listed certain promises. Among those being baptized were three or four young students, who not only paid no attention to what the pastor was reading, they took the opportunity to play among themselves — "you push me, I hit you". After three or four minutes the pastor completed his reading and the students stopped playing. One by one they were baptized. From that time on, according to custom, they were regarded as Christians.

Many churches accept new members on the principle "the more the better". That is their only concern. Some preachers urge people to join the church in the same way that a young people's group stage a recruiting drive. They speak to would-be members; they coax them; they put pressure on them. Should the one they are dealing with be a person of property or influence, they will step up their efforts to draw him into the church.

Even zealous preachers who are faithfully serving God sometimes pay more attention to quantity than to quality. They undeniably preach the gospel and urge their hearers to repent and believe the Lord. But they are satisfied if those listening to the gospel give some sign of assenting — perhaps superficially. The preacher then regards them as being saved, and they are baptized and received into the church. Yet all the while the external signs are superficial and unreliable. Some people are emotionally stirred, but only for a short period. Some are unduly influenced by others. Some are wrongly motivated. Others are not sincere. If the church relies on transitory signs, and fails to make prolonged observations, it is easy for mistakes to be made. We love these zealous preachers but we cannot be other than anxious about them. The least we can do is to seek to be faithful in offering counsel.

To sum up, then, we use the terms "Christians" and "saints" since both are found in the Bible. But what of the expression "church member"? Since it does not appear in the Bible the question arises whether we should or should not discard it? Logically we ought to discard it. However, the facts being what they are, we need this kind of expression. For in the churches today there are many who have been baptized and received into the church, and yet have not yet repented or believed in the Lord. They have not yet been born again. You may, if you like, call them Christians. But they do not belong to Christ. On the other hand, if you classify them as unbelievers they will not accept it. "In a certain year and on a certain day," they say, "we were received into a certain church. We have long attended services; we have helped the church considerably; we have made substantial contributions. So how can you say that we do not believe in Christ?"

If you call these people saints or Christians, you are describing them as what they are not. But if you describe them as unbelievers, they will not acknowledge it. In those circumstances we cannot do better than refer to them simply as church members.

Romans 1:7, 12:13, 15:25,26, 16:15
1 Corinthians 1:2, 6:12, Ephesians 1:1, 1:15,16
Philippians 1:1, 4:21,22. Colossians 1:1,2, 1:4
1 Thessalonians 3:13, 2 Thessalonians 1:10, Philemon 5:7
Hebrews 13:24, Jude 3
Revelation 5:8, 8:3,4, 13:10, 16:6, 18:24, 19:8

Perfected Saints

David Yang (Yang Shaotang)
(Eph. 4:11-16, Rom. 12:2-8)

GOD HAS RAISED up apostles, prophets, evangelists, pastors and teachers in His church, not merely that men might believe in the Lord, but "to prepare God's people for works of service, so that the body of Christ may be built up." We Christians should keep two matters clearly before us — our position and our work. Our position is not just that of a child of God, but of a member of the body of Christ. Our work is not just believing in Jesus Christ but proclaiming Jesus Christ.

We should not just be individual Christians, but should stand in our place in the church as a soldier stands in the ranks. He cannot run here and there as he pleases, but must occupy his appointed post. Further, our work is one work. Whatever our occupation, our objective is the same, as Paul clearly states "I do all things for the gospel's sake."

Each part does its work

As soon as anyone believes in the Lord he at once becomes a saint in the household of God. But it is not sufficient to become saints, we must press on to be perfected as saints. What does that imply? It means to know one's function in the House of God and to function up to the hilt in that capacity, as the Word says, "as each part does its work."

When a brother has been saved, those who minister the Word should watch for the working of the Holy Spirit in his life and, noting his particular use in the House of God, should instruct him in spiritual progress and service. See that he occupies his appropriate place, so that in his functioning there may be spontaneous expansion. And all the saints themselves should make it their business not only to believe in the Lord, but to let the Spirit work in their heart, producing concern for the House of God and for other members of the Body. Under the leading of the Lord and the direction of His servants, learn to work, learn to serve, that day by day there may be spontaneous spiritual increase in usefulness.

The church is a body

The church is a body, not a company. A company can be scattered, for its unity is that of an organization springing from a common aim, activity or advantage. But a body is not the product of organization. It is not assembled by human methods, it is a growth of life. Your hand cannot be organized on to my body, nor can my ear be organized on to your head. Neither can we collect a few persons at will and make them into a family.

The children in a family are born of the one

parents, and they have a life relationship, a blood relationship. So also is the church. It is not an organized company, but has come into being by new birth of the Spirit of God. We who are children of God have been born into the family of God, and our relationship in the body of Christ is by the operation of the Holy Spirit. Viewed separately, we are individual members; viewed collectively, we are "the body of Christ". Speaking from the standpoint of God's household, we are children of one Heavenly Father; we ought therefore to seek the Spirit's enlightenment and quickening so that we may move together as fellow-members, not only loving one another, but also serving one another.

The manifestation of function

Our use as members of the body is not determined by men, not even by the leaders of the church. While certain arrangements are necessary, such arrangements are spiritual and spontaneous. You cannot ask the hand to do duty for the foot, nor the eye to do duty for the ear. Men who are invited to act as deacons will either cumber the ground by their inactivity, or bring confusion into the church by their activity. And men who are invited to act as elders when spiritually they are not elders cannot possibly build up the body.

The function of every single member of the body manifests itself with perfect spontaneity as life develops. A baby is born with five senses and four limbs, but the use of these senses and limbs is not immediately apparent. His hands cannot grasp things, his ears cannot discern sound. But just let him grow, and the function of his members will gradually become clear. Let him grow a little more, and there will also be strength to function.

So it is also in the spiritual realm. When a person is newly saved he does not know what his use in the body is; but just let him develop and it will soon be obvious. This matter of growth to full manhood is a matter of supreme importance to the children of God. You only need to grow, and your use in the body makes itself known. If you are a child of God, you will not be saved long before, quite involuntarily, you find yourself becoming concerned about the House of God. When you see the meeting-place, you will feel it is your own; and should the lamp not be in order, you will feel uncomfortable and want to put it right. When you see all the brothers and sisters you will not only have a feeling of love for them, but will be concerned to visit the sick and comfort the distressed. And when you see the work of preaching the gospel, you will realize you have your share in testifying to the grace of God, and will want to bring your friends and relatives to hear the Word. If only you let the Holy Spirit have His way in your life your function will come to light, your strength will steadily increase, and you will spontaneously develop into a useful member of the body.

If we have been "believers" for years and it is still not clear what our ministry is, then it is questionable if we have life. If we have, there is trouble somewhere. May the Spirit of the Lord graciously enlighten us and heal us and make us all useful members, each fulfilling his own function.

The secret of growth
"Until we all reach ... the knowledge of the Son of God and become mature" (Eph 4:13). The way to maturity is by "the knowledge of the Son of God." All our gatherings, all our Bible-reading and all our praying must have this one issue — the knowledge

of the Son of God. He who has not grown in the knowledge of the Son of God has not grown at all. If I read the Word and do not grow in the knowledge of the Son of God, I have read the Word in vain. If I preach the Word and those who hear do not grow in the knowledge of the Son of God, my preaching is sheer waste of time. Our spiritual progress is entirely in terms of our progress in the knowledge of Christ.

If you come to know the holiness of Christ, you will certainly become holy. If you come to know the love of Christ, you will naturally become loving. If you come to know the self-emptying of Christ, your pride will naturally vanish. If you come to know the sacrifice of Christ your self-love will naturally go and you will be able to walk in the Spirit and not in the world. If you come to know the ministry of Christ your self-seeking will naturally end, and all your strength and time will be devoted to the things of God and to the House of God. Where there is growth in the knowledge of Christ, there is growth in everything.

The Royal Bride Of Christ

Wang Mingdao

PSALM 45, a fascinating psalm about Christ and His Bride, is a prophetic utterance that has to do with Christ as King. Two verses in the psalm are quoted almost word for word in Hebrews 1:8,9.

The psalm may be divided into two sections, the first about the king, and the second about the queen. The "royal bride" in verse 9 refers of course to the bride of Christ. "Daughter" in verse 10 also refers to the royal bride, this time before she became queen.

In the space of these two verses four charges are addressed to the daughter who is about to become the royal bride. In order to please the king, she must comply with these four injunctions and when the king is enthroned she will become the royal bride, the queen. If, on the other hand, she fails to do what she is bidden, she will risk having to forfeit her position as queen. So it is with believers. To be qualified for the position of royal bride when Christ is enthroned, is dependent on whether they obey these four commands or not.

1. Listen, O daughter...and give ear

An ear that willingly listens is an essential element in the make-up of the daughter here envisaged. But what is it to which the ear listens? Is is good music, or drama, or speech? No. It is a matter of listening to the King's words. If the daughter hopes to become the bride of the king, then obviously she must act in a way that pleases the king, for only in that way will she be acceptable to him. But if she does not listen to his words, how will she know to please him? Similarly, if a believer covets the position of the royal bride of Christ, then he or she must love the words of Christ, and listen to them with eagerness and diligence.

The more believers listen to the words of Christ, the more they will know what Christ dislikes, and the better they will be placed to avoid doing it. They will know what pleases Christ, and be better placed to cultivate those things. They will appreciate more the wonder and splendour of His promises, and so wait more patiently for Him and build up their hopes more strongly. They will appreciate the love of Christ even more, and their own love for Christ will grow stronger. With all these aspects in view, we must realize how vitally important it is for us to listen carefully to all that Christ has to say to us.

To "give ear and to consider" means to concentrate on the process of listening, to put aside all those sounds and voices that might distract us, and to listen to the words of the king with singleness of purpose. Truly to listen in this way is no easy task.

And yet, when a woman loves the king, and when she also aspires to experience what he promises, she finds it easy to act in this way. On the other hand, a person who is not related to the king and has no connection with him might find his speech interminable and unendurable. But the woman depicted here is different. The voice of the king is particularly melodious to her, and she finds it more pleasant than any other voice in the world.

Why then are the ears of many believers captivated not by the voice of Christ but by the enticing voices of the world? Why do they regard Bible reading as an unpleasant chore? It is because they have no deep love for Christ, and because they have never properly understood His promises.

Come! From today let us rouse ourselves to action. In order that we may give ear to the voice of Christ, let us jettison all those things that bear the hallmark of the world — its gain and fame and indolence and pleasures.

2. Consider!

Why is the call to "give ear" accompanied by the call to consider? It is because it is not enough simply to listen. If we do not ponder what we hear we lose a good deal of the benefit. You may drink a lot of milk every day, and you may eat a lot of food such as eggs and fish, but if you suffer from indigestion your body cannot assimilate the nutrition from what you eat and drink. Only when the food has been digested will the nourishment be distributed throughout the body, and only in that way will you gradually grow healthy and strong. Listening may be compared to the process of eating, and pondering may be compared to the process of digesting.

A believer must hide the Scriptures deeply in his heart, and in order to absorb the meaning he must deeply ponder what he reads. Only then will he be nourished spiritually, and gradually build up his spiritual health and virility. Unless he does this he cannot be as a bride who is pleasing to Christ.

Let us face it! To give ear and to listen is hard; to ponder is harder. For we can only obtain benefit from the latter by spending time and by maintaining a spirit of meditation. May God enable us to meditate, and to spend time in pondering the beautiful and marvellous words of Christ.

3. Forget your people and your father's house

What a difficult thing this is to do! What an awesome sacrifice to make! Yet here is a condition that must be fulfilled. "No one can serve two masters. Either he will hate the one and love the other, or he will be devoted to the one and despise the other" (Matt. 6:24). A strong and burning affection can have only a single focus. If the focus of our affections is the world it cannot at the same time be Christ.

It is natural for a woman to love her home, her father, her sisters and brothers, her native place. But if she aims to secure the love of her husband, she cannot do other than turn her back on everything that would hinder her following him. So long as her love for her husband is sufficiently burning and strong, she will willingly abandon all these other things. In fact it will not be a conscious difficulty for her to do so.

A believer who aspires to be related to Christ as a bride must dispossess himself of the idea that he can be attached to the world and at the same time be pleasing to Christ. For the evil world in which we are situated is in every way the enemy of Christ, and Satan constantly uses the things of the world as snares to entrap those who belong to Christ. Satan's aim is to make them forget the promises of Christ and to confine their outlook to the world; they then become tainted with unrighteousness like a profligate woman.

It is exactly at this point that many believers repeatedly encounter defeat. They listen; they even ponder; and they become familiar with both the commands and the promises of the Lord Jesus Christ. But when it comes to the pleasures of the world, they are reluctant to part with them.

But what good will it do them to make more and more money? What honour does it bring them to become more and more famous? What joy does it really bring them to indulge in the pleasures of ear and eye and mouth and stomach? What comfort do they find in the friends provided for them by a secular society? No! It is no good! Maybe to begin with these believers are half in love with Christ and half in love with the world. But gradually, as the situation develops, they love Christ less and less and the world more and more. In the end they reach the point of not loving Christ at all and only loving the world.

Let us imagine a woman who, before she marries her husband, already has another man in her life. She goes to live with this other man but still clings to the hope that the husband she married will continue to love her and to bestow on her all the things that he has promised. Such a situation would of course be ludicrous. The woman would be indulging in vain hopes. But that is exactly the position of Christians who love the world and yet retain the hope that, as the royal bride, they can still receive what the king has promised. Are not such Christians deceiving themselves?

Many believers are fully aware that sin is repugnant and that Christians ought to give it a wide berth. Yet they have failed to realize that the world and the things that belong to the world are equally repugnant, and that they too should be given a wide berth. For it has been Satan's device from the very beginning to use the world and the things in it as a means of tempting men. He has continued to use this device in an unbroken line until the present day. It remains true, that so long as a believer fails to put the world out of his mind, he will never be in a position to overcome the power of the enemy.

The apostle Paul fully understood this danger. That is why he wrote to the Corinthians as follows: "I am jealous for you with a godly jealousy. I promised you to one husband, to Christ, so that I might present you as a pure virgin to him. But I am afraid that just as Eve was deceived by the serpent's cunning, your minds may somehow be led astray from your sincere and pure devotion to Christ" (2 Cor. 11:2,3). He also wrote to the Colossians: "Since, then, you have been raised with Christ, set your hearts on things above, where Christ is seated at the right hand of God. Set your minds on things above, not on earthly things" (Col. 3:1,2). Paul also adds an explanation why we should not set our affection on earthly things: "For you died, and your life is now hidden with Christ in God" (Col. 3:3). In case we still allow ourselves to wonder whether we shall finally be any better off for refusing to set our mind on earthly things, Paul hastens to assure us: "When Christ, who is your life, appears, then you also will appear with him in glory" (Col. 3:4).

Some preachers deceive both themselves and others by proclaiming certain doctrines while they themselves can only be described as "castaways". But the apostle Paul can never be classed with preachers of that nature. He certainly taught believers to renounce the world, but he himself had first put the world behind him. He described the experience: "Whatever was to my profit I now consider loss for the sake of Christ. What is more, I consider everything a loss compared to the surpassing greatness of knowing Christ Jesus my Lord, for whose sake I have lost all things" (Phil. 3:5-11).

Notice what a big step Paul had taken. He not only turned his back on sinful things but also on things that in themselves were good. All that had previously been gain — his family, his reputation, his zeal, his own righteousness — all these he now regarded as refuse. He sought with all his heart to share in Christ's sufferings and to "become like Him in his death" (Phil. 3:10).

What lofty aspirations! Many believers are bound to look on zeal of this kind as exaggerated, and think that Paul must have been out of his mind. Such a view is due wholly to the fact that their spiritual standard is too low. The fact is, all who aspire to be royal brides of Christ ought to adopt the attitude outlined above. Paul was well aware that when love for the world begins to increase, love for Christ begins to decrease. And in order to preserve a perfect love for Christ one must accept that loss and renunciation are inevitable.

How true this is in experience! When we think over the things that normally sap our love for Christ, they are the things we most delight in. When we find our love for Christ growing cold, it is often on account of fame, wealth, glory, pleasures, friends or home and family — those things that we are most fond of? To abandon is to suffer acute loss. But by this means we qualify to know Christ as our divine and glorious bridegroom. The reward we inherit is infinitely greater than any loss that we experience.

"Forget your people and your father's house. The king is enthralled by your beauty" (Psalm 45:10,11). It was because the bride forgot her people and her father's house that the king was enthralled by her beauty. She was certainly beautiful, but if she had been unable to obey the king's instructions and forget her father's house, it would have shown that her love for the king was inadequate. Her beauty alone was insufficient to enthrall him. However, she was not only beautiful but also fervently in love with the king. That is why she could win the king's affection and the right to become the royal bride. We believers can only ask ourselves: how deep is our love for Christ?

4. *Honour him, for he is your lord*

No one's heart can ever be a blank. If the heart is not pondering one thing it is pondering something else. If it is not occupied in loving one thing it will certainly be occupied in loving something else. If it expels something old it will look for something new to take its place, otherwise the return of the old is unavoidable. The psalmist clearly has such a possibility in mind. For after instructing the woman to forget her father's house he immediately sets before her what is now the priority — to honour Christ as Lord. She is to love what he loves, to hate what he hates, to obey his commands, to serve him with all her heart and will, and to regard him as more precious than all else. Consideration for him must be greater than concern for her own life.

The king is very precious to her; she for her part is greatly cherished by the king. To the king she offers worship; the king affords her honour. She abases herself before the king, and the king, on account of this, exalts her and causes her to sit on the throne. "To him who overcomes, I will give the right to sit with me on my throne..." (Rev. 3:21).

Far too many Christians regard wealth or fame as their master and in consequence worship it. There are also Christians who regard their wives, husbands or children as their masters and as a consequence give them their worship. Such Christians are not obeying the king's commands, so how can they expect to claim the promises?

The woman chosen to be the royal bride obeys the four commands and is thus qualified to become the bride. But next comes a passage of valuable teaching. "All glorious is the princess within her chamber; her gown is interwoven with gold. In embroidered garments she is led to the king; her virgin companions follow her and are brought to you" (vs 13,14).

The royal bride's "gown is interwoven with gold" (verse 13), and "in embroidered garments she is led to the king" (verse 14). How resplendent is a gown interwoven with gold! Worn by the bride it would set forth her great beauty even more vividly. So the king is even more "enthralled by her beauty."

We must not overlook the fact, however, that those resplendent garments would only be made ready after many days of diligent and painstaking work. Nor can we have any idea how many tears were shed in the making of these embroidered garments. The embroidering of even one garment cannot be done in one or two days. The embroidery would have been done stitch by stitch and consequently would have required great patience and perseverance. Even after many days' work it would look as if not a great deal had been accomplished. So what? Should the whole thing be given up? In that event it would have been out of the question for her to see the king. The aspirant bride is thoroughly convinced that unless she exercises great patience and applies herself to the task very diligently the garment would not be completed.

Other women might spend their time in play or in feasting, but she had to sit silently and alone in the women's apartment and concentrate on her embroidery. Eventually, after many days or weeks of unremitting toil, the garment would be ready. Her patience and perseverence have produced this glorious result. She can now be led to the king and to be designated as his royal bride.

Looking back she realizes that her many days of toil have not been in vain. Her melancholy is changed into joy; her sorrow and tears have now given place to smiles; her sighs have become songs. What a happy creature she is!

The beautiful garments worn by the bride of Christ at the marriage feast are her righteous acts, as Revelation 19:7,8 shows: "Let us rejoice and be glad and give him glory! For the wedding of the Lamb has come, and his bride has made herself ready. Fine linen, bright and clean, was given her to wear. (Fine linen stands for the righteous acts of the saints.)"

If the saints aspire to become the bride of Christ and to share His glory, they must give themselves to the performance of righteous acts. Otherwise they will be brought to shame. They must ever bear in mind, however, that they will need to be as diligent and persevering in carrying this out as a bride embroidering her wedding garments. In a world so polluted and evil as ours is, to maintain the performance of righteous acts is far from easy. It means refusing to give up in spite of failures; it means getting up again after stumbling. It means overcoming the discouragement of finding that only a little progress has been made, even after working hard for many days.

The bride may be repeatedly urged by her companions to turn aside. "Let us go on an excursion!" they say. "Let us go and dance!" The flesh is weak and she is often inclined to accompany them. But she realizes that her garment will not be ready unless she perseveres. So she resolutely refuses to heed all distracting voices.

So believers must find a secluded place for prayer, for reading the Scriptures, and for meditation. Because of their refusal to drift on the currents of the world they will be disparaged, ridiculed and insulted. They will be opposed and expelled.

It is as if the bride is cut off from the world, and has no portion in the pleasures of society. In the eyes of the world she is old-fashioned, superstitious and to be pitied (though she herself is buoyed up by hope). As life goes on she sheds innumerable tears and experiences immeasurable suffering. But her diligence and patience see her through. Before long the king will return in glory and her labours will be amply rewarded. Her hopes are fulfilled and she enters the glory of Christ.

My friends! Why do you still covet the vain reputations and empty pleasures of the world? Why are you not concerned to prepare a wedding garment? Why are you unwilling to spend time in prayer and in reading your Bible? Why not pursue those righteous deeds and those superior virtues that are pleasing to Christ?

With this spiritual quest ahead of us, may God enable us all to press on diligently, patiently and perseveringly.

5

LIVING
AS
A CHRISTIAN

The pilgrim life

Min Ruji

ABRAHAM was a man chosen by God. God called him out of Ur of the Chaldees and said to him, "You must leave your native land, and tribe, and your father's home and go to the land which I will show you" (Gen. 12:1). Then God led him into Canaan and gave this promise to him, "I will give this land to your posterity as an inheritance" (Gen. 17:8).

When Abraham came to Canaan he was 75 years of age, and he lived until he was 175. During that hundred years he was greatly blessed by God. He owned many cattle, sheep and slaves.

The people of Canaan lived in buildings, but Abraham lived in tents, refusing to put up buildings for himself. It was not that he had no money, nor that he was unable to buy land. In Canaan he was in alliance with many of the heads of tribes, and after his wife's death he bought a plot of land for her burial. So it would not have been difficult for him to buy a plot of land. Nor was there any particular obstacle to putting up buildings.

In spite of this, Abraham consistently lived in tents. Why? God had promised that his descendants would be as numerous as the stars and as the sand by the sea, and had also promised to give him the whole land of Canaan. However, all these things were of the world, and Abraham knew that God was simply using them to symbolize what He was to prepare for us in heaven.

So Abraham by faith made his home in the promised land like a stranger in a foreign country; he lived in tents, as did Isaac and Jacob, who were heirs with him of the same promise" (Heb. 11: 9). It is also recorded that "All these people were still living by faith when they died. They did not receive the things promised; they only saw them and welcomed them from a distance. And they admitted that they were aliens and strangers on earth" (Hebrews 11:13).

So Abraham lived consistently as an alien and as a pilgrim. He said to himself, "I and my descendants will certainly live in tents, for my home is in heaven and not on earth. Here in this place I am but an alien and a pilgrim, so I will live the life of a pilgrim." God perceived the attitude of Abraham's heart, and what He saw was pleasing to Him.

Hebrews 11 continues, "People who say such things show that they are looking for a country of their own. If they had been thinking of the country they had left, they would have had opportunity to return. Instead, they were longing for a better country — a heavenly one. Therefore, God is not ashamed to be called their God, for he has prepared a city for them" (Heb. 11:14-16).

The Church is also called out by God
The word "church" in Chinese (*jiao-hui*) has no significance for us (literally it means a "religious

society"). But in the original it had a great deal of significance, for it refers to a body of people who have been "called out". Although they live in the world they have, by the grace of God, been called out of it, so they do not belong to it. These people constitute the church.

The road taken by Abraham and his descendants is made clear to us. "By faith Abraham, when called to go to a place he would later receive as his inheritance, obeyed and went, even though he did not know where he was going" (Heb. 11:8). That is also descriptive of the church. Each one of us who believes is called out to tread the upward path to heaven — the home that God has for us. In the light of this, so long as we are in the world we are aliens and pilgrims. We belong to the world no longer. Although, in a physical sense, our homes are in Shanghai, so far as the spirit is concerned we are travellers and pilgrims. This is in fact a great favour that God has bestowed on us.

Travelling the Road

Genesis 4 lists the descendants of Cain, giving a total of seven generations. The Bible records only their names; it does not tell us how long they lived. Chapter 5 gives a list of the descendants of Adam's third son, Seth, a total of ten generations. In this case it records not only their names but also their ages.

There is in this a lesson for us. No matter how long the descendants of Cain lived — and there must have been tens of thousands of them — they were not in God's favour. Here in China we have certain conventional greetings. When we meet an elderly gentleman we ask him, "Elderly Gentleman! May I ask what is your venerable age?" He then replies, "I have lived vainly for 70 years." This expression is not inaccurate. For whether we live to be 70 or 80, what is the value of all that we achieve during our life in the world? How much of what we have done will endure? Truly it is a case of living vainly. So in the case of the descendants of Cain the Bible makes no mention of their ages. It is quite otherwise in the case of Seth. The manner of life of Seth and his descendants was pleasing to God. They drew near to God and walked with Him. The fruits of what they did are lasting.

In the New Testament era there is also no record of how long people lived. We are not told how long Simon and Anna lived, or Mary, or Paul, or John. In fact the Bible does not tell us how long even the Lord Jesus lived. Are we to conclude, then, that their lives were lived in vain? Certainly not! In the plans and purposes of God the New Testament era represented a different economy. The situation had completedly changed. In ancient times God created man to make his abode on earth and to cover it. But man fell and became depraved. God then used the flood to destroy the world, for it had become a place of sin, debauchery and depravity. So God called out a people who were to be separated from the world with all its pleasures. He would prepare a home for them in heaven and they were to enjoy every spiritual blessing.

Thus it is written, "Then I saw a new heaven and a new earth, for the first heaven and the first earth had passed away, and there was no longer any sea. I saw the Holy City, the new Jerusalem, coming down out of heaven from God, prepared as a bride beautifully dressed for her husband" (Revelation 21:1,2). The present age will be judged, cursed and destroyed. So although we now live in the world, and it is still necessary to eat our food and to wear our clothes as people of the world, yet in the purposes of God we are blessed with all kinds of spiritual blessing in heavenly places. Our future home is a city with foundations, an eternal city.

The New Testament is not concerned to record people's ages, because God no longer emphasizes how long we live, but whether we complete our course or not. In Acts 9:25 we read about John the Baptist, "As John was completing his work..." The Bible does not tell us how long he lived, only that he completed his course. During Paul's first imprisonment he wrote to the church at Philippi pointing out that although he desired to depart and to be with Christ, "it is more necessary for you that I remain in the body." And he added, "Convinced of this I know that I will remain, and I will continue with all of you for your progress and joy in the faith..." (Phil. 1:23-26). But when he later wrote to Timothy it was in a different strain. He wrote, "I have finished the race" (2 Timothy 4:7). He had completed his allotted course and was now ready to return to his heavenly home. So there is no further talk in the New Testament about ages.

We are all "of exalted age". Do we not all possess eternal life? For us who are Christians the world is a place of schooling. The reason that God ordains that we live 30, 40, 50, 60 or even 70 years is in order that we should continue to learn — to learn the things of eternity, to learn holiness and faith and sincerity, and to learn to love as God loves. When we have learned our lessons God will receive us in our home in heaven. We shall there enter university, so to speak, and continue learning. If in primary school we do not make the progress we should in (say) arithmetic, we shall undoubtedly be worse off for it when we reach middle school. In the same way, if we do not make a point of learning in this life we shall undoubtedly be the worse off for it when we eventually reach heaven. So Christians must live in this world very positively; they must avoid wasting time lest they give offence to God.

Set your hearts on things above

Brothers and sisters! If you are clear in your mind on this point you will not be drawn into spending excessive time on the affairs of the world. David prepared an abundance of material for God's temple, and Solomon spent much time and labour on building it. But what happened to it? It survived only a few hundred years. Why did God allow it to be destroyed? Because God does not regard material edifices as particularly important in themselves. Only so long as the people inside a building love and worship God does it hold value for Him.

The two mites that the widow cast into the treasury were quickly used up, but the widow's love abides for ever. I do not know whether this chapel in which we are now worshipping will still be in existence a few years from now, but the love of the saints who worship here and their devotion to God will last for ever.

"The world and its desires pass away, but the man who does the will of God lives for ever" (1 John 2:17). It is not enough merely to understand this truth. We must ask God's help so that we may demonstrate it in the way we live. Brothers! When you go home, take another look at your equipment. Is it the house of a pilgrim, or does it suggest that you intend to stay there for a hundred years? It is by the way we live that we reveal ourselves as pilgrims. If you live as though you are going to be attached to the world for many decades, then you are living in a manner unworthy of heaven. But if, on the other hand, you live as an alien and a pilgrim, you are counted among those of whom "the world was not worthy".

Revelation 6:10 reads, "They called out in a loud voice, 'How long, Sovereign Lord, holy and true, until you judge the inhabitants of the earth and avenge our blood?'" The phrase "inhabitants of the earth" means those for whom the earth is their home in an absolute sense. Their heart is in the world, and it is on the world that they depend for their happiness. They have persecuted Christian believers, and therefore this plea arises from the persecuted ones for the Lord to avenge their blood.

Revelation 8:13 reads, "As I watched I heard an eagle that was flying in mid-air call out in a loud voice, 'Woe! Woe! Woe! to the inhabitants of the earth, because of the trumpet blast about to be sounded by the other three angels!'" It is also written, in Revelation 13:6, "He opened his mouth to blaspheme God, and to slander his name and his dwelling place and those who live in heaven." "Those who live in heaven" refers to the church of God which has been received by Him into heaven. And in verse 8 we read, "All inhabitants of the earth will worship the beast — all whose names have not been written in the book of life belonging to the Lamb that was slain from the creation of the world." From these verses we see that there are people described as living in heaven, and others described as living on earth. What are we? Are we those who live in heaven or those who live on earth?

We are located here on earth but we are among those who live in heaven. That being so, should we not pass our time on earth as pilgrims? I urge you, my brothers and sisters, to return home and to pray and examine yourselves as to whether your manner of life is the mode of pilgrims. Is your heart the heart of a pilgrim? Or is your heart completely full of the things of the world? Are you preparing for the day when the Lord will come and take you home?

Each one of us ought to demonstrate in our lives that we are aliens and pilgrims. For only in this way can we build up a thriving church, and be worthy of our standing as children of God.

A Skin of Water and a Well of Water

C K Cheng (Cheng Jigui)

WHEN ABRAHAM sent Hagar and her son into the desert (Genesis 21: 14-19), he was only able to give her "some food and a skin of water". It was obviously impossible for him to put a well on her shoulders! There are severe limits to the amount that can be carried in a skin, and if the one who depends on it takes a wrong turning, then the water will soon be used up. To be wandering in the desert without water is certainly a dangerous situation. Hagar concluded that she and her boy were doomed to die, and her heart was extremely heavy. Dying of thirst is slow and painful, and Hagar could not bear to watch her son as he was dying. So she put him under a bush and she herself sat down at a little distance. She there gave way to sobbing.

It was then that the angel of God called out to her: "What is the matter, Hagar? Do not be afraid; God has heard the boy crying." Afterwards God opened Hagar's eyes and she then perceived that there was a well of water nearby. "So she went and filled the skin with water and gave the boy a drink."

Now, will you all please take notice! The well of water did not suddenly drop down from heaven. Nor was it located a long way away. It was in fact quite near. If the mother and her son had died of thirst it would not have been because there was no water within reach, but because they had not seen the water that was there. That would have been truly tragic.

In a time of famine many people die of hunger due to no fault of their own. But when people die of hunger when there is food available, it is nothing short of tragic. It would be quite inexplicable.

Our Lord Jesus Christ provides the living water which is available for us all. The Lord Jesus said, "Whoever drinks the water I give him will never thirst. Indeed, the water I give him will become in him a spring of water welling up to eternal life." Alas! Many people are facing the living water and yet they have not seen it, so they do not come and drink it.

Today the church is dry. It is not a question of living water, but a question of sight. It was for this reason that the apostle Paul prayed for the Ephesians "that the eyes of your heart may be enlightened in order that you may know the hope to which he has called you, the riches of his glorious inheritance in the saints" (Eph 1: 17,18).

My friends! During this Convention we have been daily meditating on the Word. If, in spite of our preaching and praying, our eyes have not been enlightened, and if we have not been drinking of the living water that Jesus provides for us, then at the most we have merely made ourselves a little more familiar with certain passages of Scripture. In other words, we have received only a skinful of water and nothing more. For just as Abraham could give no more than a skinful of water to Hagar, so what a preacher can give us of himself amounts to no more than a skinful of water. If we want to obtain a well or spring of living water, we must understand that this is beyond the power of man. It is something for which we need the enlightenment of the Holy Spirit. Only when our eyes are opened to see Jesus, and when we have Him to live in our hearts, then a supply of living water is ensured.

One of the responsibilities of a Bible School is to help students know Jesus more and more profoundly, so that they are able themselves to drink the living water He provides. If a Bible School simply helps students to complete their academic studies and nothing more, and the students simply study the Bible without being led by it to know the Lord more deeply and to drink the living water, then what they receive from their teachers is nothing more than a skinful of water. In the end they will still be in danger of dying of thirst.

This is also applicable to Bible Conventions. Their aim is not just for Christian workers to meet together, but for those attending to see Jesus and partake of the living water that He provides. There are indeed those who appropriate this living water. But there are inevitably some who simply listen to certain lectures and go no further. Thus all they do is carry away with them a skinful of water.

The water in the skin is static. The water in the spring is always fresh and always welling up. That is how our spiritual life should be. Is it in fact like this? Is it static? Or ever overflowing? The answer to this question will demonstrate whether what we have been drinking is limited to a skin of water, provided only by men, or whether it is a spring of water provided for us by the Lord Jesus.

The Risen Christ

Wang Mingdao

A WELL-KNOWN elderly church leader was the visiting speaker at a Bible class. In the course of the class one of the students stood up and asked, "Did the resurrection of Christ really take place?"

The elderly leader replied, "If you believe that Christ really rose from the dead, then you may say that it was a reality. But if you do not believe it, then you may say that He did not really rise. Actually, the resurrection of Jesus is not an important matter. The important elements in Christianity are the character and teaching of Christ, and the pattern He set of service and sacrifice. So long as we stress these things we shall develop the moral quality of our own lives and also bring benefit to society and to the world."

On hearing this leader's line of reasoning I was very grieved. Is the resurrection of Christ indeed of no particular importance? On the contrary, it is the very centre of our gospel.

1. Since Christ has risen from the dead we have an authentic Saviour
The preaching of the Lord Jesus Himself and the witness of the apostles, as they are recorded in the Bible, combine to declare that Jesus is the Christ,

that He is appointed by God and that He is the Saviour of the world. He sacrificed His life on the cross in order to be the propitiation for our sin. Thus all who believe in Him may be assured that their sins are forgiven and that they inherit eternal life. They are justified by faith.

Thank God! He has given us clear evidence of the resurrection of Christ in that He opened the tomb and with great power raised Him from the dead. In so doing He demonstrated that Christ was truly the Son of God (Rom.1:1-4), and the Lamb of God who takes away the sin of the world. The resurrection showed that the sin offering was accepted, with the result that all who believe in Him experience forgiveness (Acts 10:38-43) and participate in His salvation. From Adam until the present, where will you find a man who, after dying, has risen from the dead and never died again? That is only true of the Lord Jesus Christ who was so appointed by God. For of all men it is only the Son of God, the Lord Jesus Christ, who cannot be bound by death or the tomb. Life abundant has its source in Him, and He bestows that life on all who put their trust in Him. He who once lived on earth and there preached the doctrine of salvation now lives in heaven where He exercises His power to save sinners.

Suppose I have a friend who has promised that in a year's time he will obtain certain valuable presents for me. Would I not await his gifts expectantly? But what if my friend becomes ill and dies before the year has elapsed? Obviously he cannot fulfil his promise, and my hopes will collapse. When the Lord Jesus was on earth He promised repeatedly that He would save all who believe in Him and bestow on them eternal life (John 3:16). They would become the children of God (John 1:12). But what if Jesus dies? His promises would fall to the ground, for obviously the dead can no longer fulfil their promises. We thank God, however, that although Jesus died, in three days He rose again. And He will never die again. The Christ who never dies will of course be able to fulfil His promises.

2. Since Christ has risen we now have a victorious leader to follow

It is the will of God that all who are redeemed by Christ should not only be justified and saved but that they should be overcomers. As overcomers they would merit a glorious reward. An overcomer is one who has served in the front line and there defeated the enemy. For of necessity every one who belongs to Christ must be involved in fierce and bitter battles. We are attacked by enemies without and within. The one who attacks from outside is the evil one who is wholly cunning and cruel and who has authority in the air (Eph.6:12). The enemy within is sin in the flesh (Rom 7:14-24).

When we consider that the enemy is so strong, while we are so weak, we may truly wonder whether there can be any hope of victory at all. But God opens our eyes to see that the Lord Jesus Christ has already won a great victory. He has subdued the devil who holds the power of death (Heb.2:14) and has shown us that He has already overcome the world (John 16:33). "To him that overcomes," He said, "I will give the right to sit with me on my throne, just as I overcame and sat down with my Father on his throne" (Rev.3:21).

When a victorious general returns from battle he is

greeted with appropriate rewards. The rewards incidentally provide evidence of his victories. It is the same with Christ. After Christ rose He was received into heaven where He sits at the right hand of God (Mark 16:19), and was "crowned with glory and honour because He suffered death" (Heb.2:9).

Because Jesus has risen from the dead and is victorious, we know that those who are joined to him are also victorious. It is true that we are weak, but since Christ has risen from the dead we can be transformed and made strong. Although we sometimes stumble we are not without hope of getting up again. With Christ as our leader we have no enemy that cannot be overcome. Through the risen Christ we can be more than conquerors. Let us then put our trust in the Lord. Let us lift up our eyes and look to Him.

3. Since Christ has risen we have a great High Priest who is both faithful and compassionate

After Christ had ascended to heaven He assumed the most important ministry of the Great High Priest. His is a priesthood that does not change. "The Lord has sworn and will not change His mind: 'You are a priest for ever, in the order of Melchizedek'" (Psalm 110:4, Heb.5:1-10).

Believers often grow weak, and stumble, and suffer defeat; they sometimes become disheartened and lose hope; they are grieved when they sin and perhaps give way to a feeling that they have forfeited God's blessing. Yet they really do not need to despair in this way. For the duties of the High Priest have been determined with just such needs in mind. This provision is clearly set out in the book of

Hebrews: "Every high priest is selected from among men and is appointed to represent them in matters related to God, to offer gifts and sacrifices for sins. He is able to deal gently with those who are ignorant and are going astray, since he himself is subject to weakness" (Heb.5:1,2). Have we not here a great source of comfort?

The weaknesses and failures of believers truly abound, but Christ is well acquainted with them. For He has been "tempted in every way, just as we are — yet without sin" (Heb.4:15). He knows well how fierce are our temptations and how we are hampered by weaknesses of the flesh. But He also knows that those who love the Lord have no desire to fall into sin, and that it is because of the weakness of the flesh that they are unable to overcome these fierce temptations. So the Lord does not abandon us. The same love that was manifested when He shed His blood for us is now expressed in His sympathy as He pleads with the Father on our behalf. The priceless offering He made, once for all, is enough to cover all our transgressions.

It is for this reason that the apostle John wrote: "If we confess our sins, he is faithful and just and will forgive our sins and purify us from all unrighteousness" (1 John 1:8,9). The apostle then tells us how we may be forgiven and cleansed. "If anybody does sin, we have one who speaks to the Father in our defence — Jesus Christ, the Righteous One" (1 John 2:1).

We must be careful that we do not misunderstand this verse. There are some who infer from it that a believer may sin with impunity. But this is not so. If one who is called a believer desires to sin and looks for opportunities to sin, and regards committing sin as something to be enjoyed, then it is quite clear that he has not yet been saved. He must repent and believe in Christ.

But having said that, what a precious truth it is that although we frequently fail and suffer defeat, we can still come again into the presence of God. Although we stumble we can get up again. So if you are defeated through the weakness of the flesh, on no account lose hope or come to the conclusion that you have been cast off for ever. You should immediately bring your failures and transgressions to your great High Priest and look to Him for deliverance. "Such a high priest meets our need — one who is holy, blameless, pure, set apart from sinners, exalted above the heavens" (Hebrews 7:26).

It is recorded in the Old Testament that when the High Priest entered the holy place he carried with him into the presence of God the names of the twelve tribes of Israel. What a valuable truth is here enshrined! Sometimes we feel incapable of engaging in prayer and it seems to us almost as if our communication with God has been broken. But through the intercession of our Great High Priest we experience once again God's grace and favour. Even though we ourselves may drift away from God, He never leaves God's presence. Our prayers at times may be interrupted, but His intercession is never interrupted. His prayer, moreover, is powerful and effective. So there is no break in the supply of God's grace. That is why, though we go astray, we may return to the rightful path; although we stumble, we may rise; although we are taken captive by the enemy, we can still regain our freedom. That is all due to the work for us of our Great High Priest. How marvellous!

4. Since Christ has risen we have a Friend who is ever-present

Do you remember the promise that the Lord Jesus once made to His disciples? He said, "I tell you that .... where two or three come together in my name, there am I with them" (Matt.18:19). What a joy it is for us that our Lord Jesus meets with His disciples like this! The Lord Jesus also promised that He would be with His disciples until the end of the age (Matt.28:18-20).

Just as the Lord Jesus was with His disciples in days of old, so He is with them today. He was with them in both peace and danger. His presence with them was never affected by variations of time or place, and it made no difference whether they were rich or poor, high or low, wise or stupid, strong or weak. The Lord Jesus is absolutely faithful and in no circumstances will He go back on His promises.

But the question inevitably arises, on what grounds can we base our reliance on these promises? On the grounds that the Lord Jesus did not remain in the grave but rose from the dead, and that He is alive for ever and ever. "I am the Living One," He assures us, "I was dead, and behold I am alive for ever and ever!" (Rev.1:8).

Grief and sorrow and weeping are the common experiences of many believers. Are you misunderstood, ridiculed and opposed as a consequence of obeying God? Are there times when you suffer and no one seems to be aware of your grievances or come to comfort you? Perhaps, because you are unwilling to follow the crowd, your path is a lonely one. Perhaps the members of your family are annoyed with you and your friends seem to avoid you. So your lot is a lonely one. Or maybe you have some disease and even after many months you have still not regained your health. Maybe you have lost someone very dear to you, or something has emptied your life of its meaning. As a result of experiences like this you have shed many tears and uttered many sighs.

My friends! Here is news to comfort you. Listen to the words of the Lord who is now risen: "If anyone loves me, he will obey my teaching. My Father will love him, and we will come to him and make our home with him" (John 14:23).

So do not be anxious about the misfortunes you encounter. It is only necessary for you to love the Lord Jesus. He will comfort you when you have griefs and when false accusations are made against you. When you are persecuted He will strengthen you. When you are lonely He will go with you. When you are bereaved He will be near you. The persecution that you have suffered for His Name, as well as the losses of your possessions, are all perfectly known to Him. And when His glory is revealed He will reward you abundantly.

As a believer you are sometimes placed in difficult and dangerous circumstances; you may even be threatened and attacked by evil men. What then is your reaction? Do you waver and deny the name of Christ? Or do you courageously bear witness? Never forget, when confronted by danger, that He who is in you is greater than he who is in the world. Remember the word that comforted and strengthened the apostle Paul when the Lord spoke to him in a vision: "Do not be afraid, keep on speaking, do not be silent. For I am with you" (Acts 18:9,10).

5. Since Christ has risen we have a priceless hope for the future

Before Jesus took leave of His disciples He gave them a promise. He said, "I am going... to prepare a place for you. And... I will come back and take you to be with me that you also may be where I am" (John 14:2,3). The apostle Paul opened up the meaning of these promises, especially in his letter to the Corinthians: "Listen, I tell you a mystery. We will not all sleep, but we will all be changed — in a flash, in the twinkling of an eye, at the last trumpet. For the trumpet will sound, the dead will be raised imperishable, and we will be changed. For the perishable must clothe itself with the imperishable, and the mortal with immortality" (1 Cor.15:51-53).

Suppose Christ, after dying, had not risen from the dead. All these promises would have been empty. These precious truths would have been nothing more than wild talk. But thank God! He has already raised Christ from the dead and caused Him to ascend to heaven. How can we doubt the promises of His return? We ourselves shall be raised from the dead and utterly transformed. Listen again! "For as in Adam all die, so in Christ all will be made alive. But each in his own turn: Christ the firstfruits; then, when he comes, those who belong to him" (1 Cor.15:20, 23).

A man from the cold northern part of China made his first trip, with a friend, to the warmer south. In their travels they came across a certain kind of fruit tree, and the visitor from the north asked his friend what the fruit was called and what it tasted like. Although his friend described the taste so far as possible, the visitor could not even imagine what it was like. The friend would like to have given him some of the fruit to taste. But it was still early in the season and it was not yet ripe. Then he discovered that on one of the branches there was just one big red fruit, the first ripe fruit on the tree. The friend picked the fruit and gave it to his visitor. He took a bite and discovered it was most delicious. This should have been enough, but he told his friend that until the rest of the fruit on the tree ripened he would not really know what it tasted like.

Such a reaction is, of course, laughable. For naturally the fruit to ripen later would taste just the same as the single piece of fruit that had ripened early.

In the same way, although we have not yet seen any saints who have been raised from the dead and although our own bodies have not yet been transformed, we are nevertheless fully persuaded that the promise of ultimate resurrection is genuine. This is because Christ has first risen. He is the firstfruit. Because He Himself has first risen, been transformed and received up into glory, we know that we also shall experience this, as He has promised. Had Christ Himself not risen there would be a question mark over the promises of our resurrection. However, Christ has risen. So if we still entertain doubts about our own future resurrection, we are like the visitor from North China. Would we not also be a laughing-stock?

Beloved friends! Since we know how excellent are the promises that God has given us, let us receive them with grateful hearts, regard lightly the perishable pleasures and glory of the world we live in, and seek with singleness of purpose those things that can never be lost or forfeited. Let us arise! Forgetting what is behind and straining towards what is ahead, let us press on towards the goal to win the prize for which God has called us heavenwards in Christ Jesus!

Is This The Way You Pray?

Wang Mingdao

O GOD, I plead with you to enable me to learn patience, but do not allow me to encounter provoking circumstances!

Enable me to be meek, but do not allow people to arouse my anger!

Enable me to grow humble, but do not allow people to despise me!

Enable me to love my enemies, but do not allow people to become hostile toward me!

Enable me to forgive people, but do not allow people to offend me!

Enable me to be willing to give way, but do not allow people to attack me!

Enable me to be courageous, but do not allow me to meet adverse circumstances!

Enable me to trust you fully, but do not allow me to encounter difficulties and dangers!

Enable me to be diligent, but do not give me vexatious work!

Enable me to be faithful, but do not entrust me with heavy responsibilities!

Purge away the dross, but do not allow me to pass through the fire!

Enable me to be an overcomer, but do not allow me to be attacked by Satan!

Enable me to endure persecution, but do not

allow people to revile me or oppose me!

Enable me to be willing to deny myself for others, like the Lord Jesus denied Himself, but do not allow me to suffer loss!

Enable me not to love the world, but do not take away my reputation or my wealth or my friends!

Enable me to recognize more of my own faults and failings, but do not allow anyone to point them out or to rebuke me for them!

Enable me to be obedient unto death, like the Lord Jesus, but do not allow me to experience the cross!

Have you ever heard prayers that can be summed up in this way? Have you never prayed like this? I have to confess that I myself have done so.

For example, I recently met a Christian lady whose family were not of one mind with her, and in fact constantly oppressed her. Because of this she almost lost hope. "I no longer dare to pray," she said. "I once called upon God to enable me to endure, and I expected that the storm would abate. But in fact it happened otherwise. One morning I asked the Lord to teach me patience, but on that very day I was put in a situation that was very hard to endure. 'Surely,' I thought, 'it is better not to pray. The more you pray the worse the situation becomes'."

"Surely this is precisely a case of God hearing your prayer," I said to her. "Did you not plead with Him to help you learn patience? If nobody had bothered you, and all the circumstances were favourable, where would you have learned patience? You asked God to teach you patience, and the adverse circumstances that you experienced were surely His answer to your prayer."

Many Christian believers have this same viewpoint. When God acts in answer to their prayer, they blame Him for treating them as He does. For the most part it is because they have not fully grasped God's will or comprehended His ways.

We ought to recognize that even the adverse circumstances which we dislike all arise as a result of God's appointment. Even when we do not call on Him for help He still acts in love to edify us. How much more will He do so when we call on Him?

God allows us to be provoked in order that we may learn meekness. He brings us low, to the place where people look down on us, so that we may learn humility. We ask Him for help to love our enemies and He allows people to treat us with hostility. We ask help to forgive people, and He allows people to give us offence. And so on.

So, the various circumstances that we meet — adverse as many are — constitute the text-books and laboratories that God uses to teach us the most valuable lessons. Without these things we should be unable to grow strong, experienced or mature; we would never reach our objectives.

Many times, when we pray, we do not know what we are asking for. We invariably hope that we shall obtain what we seek. It is true that we desire to learn the deepest spiritual lessons, but the problem is that all too often we are unwilling to take our place in God's classroom. If we shun the classroom, how long will it be before we graduate?

May God open our eyes to recognize our previous ignorance and mistakes. May He enable us not only to take our places in the classroom that He has set aside for us, but also so to apply our minds that we may learn joyfully all the valuable lessons that He would teach us!

What Kind Of Friends?

Wang Mingdao

NO MATTER who you are, you cannot avoid being influenced by the friends you make. If you are closely associated with people who are devout and serious-minded, then you will unconsciously become devout and serious-minded like them. But if you are closely associated with people who are depraved and whose thoughts are unholy, then your whole life will unconsciously become degenerate. If your friends are exasperating and hot-tempered it will be easy for you to develop characteristics that will bring friction between you and other people. But if your friends are of a meek disposition, it will be easier for you to be tolerant and patient. If your friends are diligent, you will learn to work hard. But if your friends are idle then your own life is in danger of being squandered. If your friends are courageous, you yourself will grow bolder and stronger daily. But if your friends are cowardly, you yourself may waver when things are against you.

If you habitually converse with believers who are strong in the faith, your own faith will grow stronger. But if you consort with those who are full of doubt, then it will be easier for your own faith to be shaken. The Bible teaches us that "He who walks with the wise grows wise, but a companion of fools suffers harm" (Proverbs 13:20).

Christians must keep company with those who love the Lord. By exhorting and encouraging each other they can help to develop each other's spiritual life. Admittedly you cannot expect to have a large group of friends of this nature, but you can at least have a few. When A is weak, then B and C can strengthen him. When B stumbles, then A and C can lift him up. When C is discouraged, then A and B can encourage him. All are linked together as a group so that each individual may stand firm. For if all act separately from each other it will not be easy to avoid division and dissension, and one by one they may break down.

So if we want to be robust and vigorous Christians we not only need to be joined in fellowship to the Lord but also in fellowship with one another.

Bring Jesus Into Your Home!

Marcus Cheng

CHRISTIANITY is peculiarly the religion of the home. That is why the home is mentioned so frequently in the Bible. When the Lord Jesus lived on earth he was often to be found in people's homes. We are told that after Jesus had healed the man possessed by an evil spirit, He "went with James and John to the home of Simon and Andrew" (Mark 1:29). Then Luke 10:38 tells us that "As Jesus and his disciples were on their way, he came to a village where a woman named Martha opened her home to him." When another demon-possessed man had been healed he begged to accompany Jesus. But Jesus would not let him. He said, "Go home to your family and tell them how much the Lord has done for you, and how he has had mercy on you" (Mark 5:19). We also frequently read of the home in the letters of Paul and Peter and John.

One of the greatest needs in China today is for Christian homes. The God of many Christians is restricted to their places of worship. Their God and their faith have never been brought into the home. What it amounts to is that *they have never welcomed Jesus into their home*. They pray in the church building, but not at home. They read the Bible in the church building but not at home. This situation prevails not only with many ordinary believers but also with many preachers, whose manner of life should be a pattern for others.

I once heard a preacher publicly confess that he had not yet welcomed Jesus into his home, and that he had never conducted family prayers. What did characterize their home was constant quarelling between husband and wife. Christians who do not take their Christianity into their homes are hypocritical. The word "hypocrisy" had the original meaning, in the Greek, of taking part in theatrical performances. An actor leaves his home and then enters the theatre and mounts the stage. He wears a mask. Whether he laughs or cries, all is feigned, all is pretence. It is simply a performance for people to look at. When the performance is over the actor discards his mask and his dressing up; he ceases to smile. When he returns to his home his words and actions are completely different.

The Christian life of some believers is like that. In the context of the place of worship they are dignified and courteous; they speak of love and righteousness and virtue. But when they return home their treatment of their parents and wives and children only serves to reveal their true nature. They are niggardly; they are proud; they give way to temper.

During a revival meeting one of the church members wept and prayed. Before the meeting was over he got up and left. I heard afterwards that he had returned home to express his regret to his wife for his past carrying-on in the home. He had been habitually discourteous, offensive, and short-tempered.

So it is of vital importance that Christians should welcome the Lord Jesus into their homes. He should be the honoured guest; He should be the Head. We should obey Him, reverence Him and trust Him. There should be nothing in the home that Jesus may not see, no words that Jesus may not listen to. The home should be filled by the Spirit of Jesus.

There are still old habits and ungodly practices in the home that ought to be changed. And we ought to look to Jesus for the zeal and courage to change them. Much of the trouble in the home is due to these changes having never been made. For example, some parents insist on arranging marriages for their children when the children are physically immature and not yet self-supporting. These early marriages result in many families becoming poor and going into debt. It means that some become corrupt and resort to dishonesty. It is in the home of Christians that reform should begin.

The bad habits that grow up in homes are too numerous to list. But whenever people invite the Lord Jesus into their home they will set about getting them changed.

It is important that our homes should be neat and clean, to be places where we can relax. But the most important thing, of course, is neither the building nor the furniture; it is the spirit of Christ. Between all the members of the family — parents and children, husbands and wives, brothers and sisters — there should be mutual respect, mutual toleration, and mutual love. These qualities are best developed when there are religious practices in the home. Wherever you have prayer, the reading of the Bible and worship of God, there will be a spiritual atmosphere and the family can cultivate love and harmony.

So it is most important to develop a practice of worship in the home. No matter how weighty are your responsibilities in the church, how zealous you are for the preservation of true doctrine, how much you love your country and care for society, if you neglect your own home and fail to carry out your obligations to your relatives, then all these things lose their value.

I recall the time in our home, before we believed in Christ, when it was our practice to worship idols. Whenever there was anything auspicious, some event to be celebrated, or bereavement had occurred, we would be sure to worship these gods. On believing in the Lord we gave up the worship of idols. The question then arose: "Now that we are Christians is it not even more important for us to worship the true God?" We concluded that this was indeed so. So whenever there is a marriage or a bereavement, or some festival, we ought to read the Bible and worship God. More than that, there should be family worship in every Christian home at least once a day.

When there are non-believers in the family we can influence them to believe by maintaining the practice of prayer and Bible-reading. A certain church member had been a Christian for many years but he had never received Jesus into his home, and no arrangements had been made for family worship. One day he heard a pastor preach on the relevance of family worship and he was greatly moved. That evening for the first time the family met for worship. Husband and wife read the Bible together and prayed together. Up to that time his father, who was an opium smoker, had never attended any place of worship. But that evening, while he was smoking opium, he observed his son and daughter-in-law praying. This greatly impressed him and he put aside his opium pipe to join them. When they prayed together he was much affected and began to weep over his sins. From that day he gave up smoking opium and began to learn about the Christian faith.

Family worship and the integrity of the family are closely related. When parents habitually pray and read the Bible, they inevitably influence their children. But if we parents are characterized by bad habits, whether in speech or action, we shall become stumbling blocks to the children. In that case, no matter how good their pastor or teachers are, it will be almost impossible to nullify the bad influence of the parents.

The situation is even more lamentable when a preacher or pastor is dissatisfied with his calling and constantly complains of his hard lot in front of the children. This could discourage them from becoming preachers themselves and thus adversely affect the future of the church in China. It is essential that the churches in China be fed and nourished by Christian homes.

The influence of a Christian home is indeed powerful beyond measure. A visitor went to call at the home of a well-known preacher, and the door was answered by one of the children. "Is your father at home?" asked the caller. "Yes, father is at home," replied the child, "but just at the moment he is in his room talking to Jesus." This is the kind of family culture we need in our churches today.

A mother took her small daughter to their place of worship, and that day the pastor preached on the need for Christian homes. "Alas!" he said, "some mothers neglect the spiritual education of their children. For instance some mothers do not pray with their children at bedtime." He then mentioned other omissions in family life. The small daughter listened attentively and afterwards she commented to her mother, "Mama! The pastor was talking about you, wasn't he?" The mother was so convicted that she confessed her shortcomings before God, and from that time on she was a different mother entirely.

Of Whom Will The Son Of Man Be Ashamed?

Wang Mingdao

"IF ANYONE is ashamed of me and my words in this adulterous generation, the Son of Man will be ashamed of him when he comes in his Father's glory with the holy angels" (Mark 8:38).

The greatest hope of Christians, and their greatest prospective joy, is that when the Lord Jesus comes again in glory they will receive His commendation and praise. But some Christians will not only fail to receive His commendation, they will even be numbered among those of whom the Lord Jesus is ashamed. Any Christian who merits such treatment is greatly to be pitied. But this is the consequence of being ashamed of the Lord and his words. It is because the Lord is unwilling to see His disciples inherit such misfortune that he gives them this warning in advance. They can then take steps to avert it.

Why must those who are ashamed of the Lord and His words suffer such consequences? If we ponder the matter for a minute we shall soon understand that this is not unreasonable. Where shall we find anyone in all the world who loves us more than the Lord Jesus loves us, who deals with us more graciously than He does, who has given up more for us, and endured greater suffering for us than He has?

Whenever we receive favours from other people we express our appreciation to them; not to do so is to show ingratitude. The Lord Jesus loved us and sacrificed Himself for us; for our sakes He endured the most bitter suffering. In the light of all that shall we — in order to save our faces — be ashamed of Him and His words in this sinful and adulterous generation? How far shall we allow ourselves to be carried by our ingratitude? People who show ingratitude are surely among the meanest people around. So if our Lord Jesus in the Father's glory is ashamed of people like this, can it be regarded as unreasonable? Actually, when that day comes, it will hardly be necessary for the Lord Jesus to be ashamed of them. They will be greatly ashamed of themselves, and will have no "face" to meet the Lord.

Any Christian who is ashamed of the Lord is clearly one who loves himself far more than he loves the Lord. He is prepared to grieve the Lord but he has no intention of grieving himself. His own "face" and reputation and honour and profit mean more to him than the Lord Jesus Himself. Should it be possible to confess the name of the Lord and at the same time enhance his own happiness and glory, then he will do so. But that would not be due to love for the Lord; it would simply be a case of making use of the Lord. But should the day come when to confess the Lord would involve him in loss, he will soon think of a way to get out of it.

When people confess the Lord in times of calm they are not necessarily motivated by love. But when they confess the Lord in times of opposition, when the name of the Lord is hated, we may be quite sure that they truly love the Lord.

When a person encounters trouble and becomes the butt of insults or the target of persecution, those who stand by him in spite of everything demonstrate that they are genuine friends. Unfortunately friends of this calibre are as rare as morning stars. It is even more lamentable that the genuine friends of the Lord Jesus Christ are so rare. When people claim to love Christ, but do not really do so in their hearts, it is in no way unjust that the Lord in His glory should be ashamed of them.

But there is more to it than this. When a Christian is ashamed of his Lord it usually means that he is guilty of other sins in addition. He will tell lies, or cheat, or use unworthy methods to obscure the fact that he is a Christian. He may even blaspheme the Lord. He is indeed capable of betraying the Lord and of betraying those who love Him. If a person like that does not soon repent and confess his sin, his heart may well become harder and harder with every day that passes. How can it be unreasonable for the Lord to be ashamed of a person like that?

We must be careful, however, that we do not err in the other direction. For even if the Lord is ashamed of us it does not mean that He discards us, or that we forfeit the life that we have become heir to through faith. When a person repents and believes in the Lord he obtains salvation and inherits eternal life, and this can never be taken from him. No matter how weak believers become, no matter how they stumble or even deny their Lord, their salvation cannot be affected. What it does mean is that we forfeit the glorious reward that the Lord has prepared for those who love Him.

It may be that among those who read this message are some who through a moment's weakness have experienced defeat in this way. If that is so, I counsel you not to lose hope. The Lord still delays His return; there is still time to repent. Remember! It was because of a moment's weakness that Peter three times denied His Lord. But when he heard the crowing of the cock he remembered what Jesus had previously said to him, and he immediately repented. He chided himself and went out and wept bitterly. As a result of repenting in this way he was restored. Not only did the Lord forgive him, but it was to Peter that the Lord first revealed Himself after His resurrection. What a comfort and encouragement this was! Afterwards, as the Lord again used him, he became an outstanding and triumphant warrior.

Although Peter had stumbled he was able to get up and be restored through forgiveness to favour. That was why the Lord could use him again so mightily, and why Peter could still qualify for the crown of glory. Any believer who has stumbled may repent in the same way and be similarly restored. So if you have stumbled and suffered defeat, all that you need to do is to turn to the Lord in repentance and sorrow, and He will enable you to rise again. You will not only be able to confess the name of the Lord before men, you will be able, for the Lord, to endure both ridicule and persecution. Like Peter your weakness will be transformed into strength, and your defeats will be turned into victories.

6 FACING RESPONSIBILITIES

Wells Without Water

Marcus Cheng

"THESE PEOPLE are wells without water, mists driven along by a storm, men for whom the dense darkness has been reserved," (2 Pet. 2:17, Weymouth).

1. What are wells without water?
In the apostolic churches, as today, there were false teachers as there are false teachers today, who covertly brought in harmful heresies. The apostle Peter called them wells without water. Although they supplied no water they were still called wells, so it was a case of the wells having a name without the reality.

In Acts 9 the followers of Christ are designated disciples, (those) who belonged to the Way, saints, those who call on the Lord's name, and brothers. In Acts 11:26 another designation may be found — Christians. The question we must ask ourselves is this: Do the designation and the reality harmonize?

I recall an English brother telling me of an

occasion when he was walking down a street in China, and the children called out "Foreign devil!" He commented to me, "I asked myself whether my actions were reminiscent of the devil. When they call me 'devil', does the name correspond with reality?" He then told me of another occasion when the children called out "Jesus!", and he again examined himself. To what extent was he really like Jesus?

Wells without water are those that have a reputation without the substance. On the outside they look like wells, but they are without water. Today as we all sing together in this chapel we can see one another's outward appearance very clearly. From the outward appearance we can detect no essential differences. But what God sees is the heart. We may appear to be wells, as it were, but are we wells that function?

Water symbolizes salvation. The prophet Isaiah says: "Come, all you who are thirsty, come to the waters." Isaiah was urging people to be saved, and he went on: "Seek the Lord while he may be found; call on him while he is near. Let him turn to the Lord, and he will have mercy on him, and to our God, for he will freely pardon" (Isa. 55: 6,7). The Lord Jesus, in conversation with the woman of Samaria, made this claim: "Whoever drinks the water I give him will never thirst. Indeed, the water I give him will become in him a spring of water welling up to eternal life" (John 4:14).

These passages refer to the salvation of God. "Wells without water" is an apt description of church members who are still unsaved.

The Lord Jesus also said, "If a man is thirsty, let him come to me and drink. Whoever believes in me, as the Scripture has said, streams of living water will flow from within him. By this he meant the Spirit, whom those who believed in him were later to receive" (John 7:37-39).

The description "wells with water" and "wells without water" may also be applied to preachers. Those who have been filled with the Spirit and preach the Word are endued with power from on high. They are like wells with an abundant supply of water, from whose inmost being flows a stream of living water. On the other hand there are preachers who preach what is biblical, but in dependence on oratory and learning. Their words contain no message. So the Holy Spirit does not work with them. Their preaching is void of power. They are wells without water.

The tragedy is that wells without water not only fail to bring any benefit, they are actually harmful. Such preachers act deceitfully. They give people the impression that in a spiritual sense they are wells; but the wells contain no water. This can only cause deep disappointment. People bring their vessels from afar, as it were, but when they expect to draw water they find there is none in the well. They return to their homes with a feeling of having been let down.

There are, of course, waterless wells that are known by people living nearby to be waterless. However that passersby, ignorant of a well's exist- ence, may find themselves falling into it. Thus a well without water becomes a pitfall. [Here there is a play on words: well = jing, pitfall = xian-jing.] In the past when false teachers in the churches spread heresy, they injured both themselves and other people. The apostle Jude wrote, "These men are blemishes at your love feasts, eating with you without the slightest qualm — shepherds who feed only themselves. They are clouds without rain, blown along by the wind; autumn trees without fruit and uprooted — twice dead. They are wild waves of the sea, foaming up their shame; wandering stars, for whom blackest darkness has been reserved for ever" (Jude 12, 13).

Let us come back to the present day. We may well use the expression "unbelieving faction" to describe liberals. For just like the people described in Jude, preachers of liberalism do injury both to themselves and other people. Those who look up to them are not only disappointed; they may even stumble and fall into the pit.

2. What are wells with water?

Wells with water may be classified in three ways. The first kind is shallow, depending entirely on rainwater. Whenever it rains the well gathers a little water, but because the well is not deep it dries up within a few days. It is without a spring to keep it supplied.

The second kind is somewhat deeper, and the volume of water it collects is appreciably bigger. Nevertheless, when a substantial amount of water has been drawn off this also becomes dry.

The third kind has the greatest depth. More than that, it is connected with springs. Wells of this kind are never exhausted, no matter how much water you draw out. No matter how much is used, there is always more available. No matter how hot the weather is, you can always find water in the well.

Near the main entrance of this Bible school there is a well which at one time was little more than ten feet deep. Whenever it rained a certain amount of water collected in the well, but within a few days it would dry up. It was totally inadequate to meet the needs of the establishment. We then engaged work-men to make the well thirty or forty feet deeper. This meant that the supply of water was appreciably increased, and it was clearer. For normal needs it was quite sufficient, but at a time of drought, when there was no rain for an extended period, we realized that it was still not good enough.

However, in the Bible school grounds there was another well that had first been dug to a depth of twenty or thirty feet, and was later deepened to fifty or sixty feet, where the water was more abundant. However, we were still not satisfied and we in-creased the depth to more than one hundred feet. Suddenly we encountered a spring, and the water then poured out in great profusion. The men digging the well made their way quickly to the surface, and in a very short time the well was full of water. As a result, during the past ten years or so, no matter how dry the weather or how many people make use of the water, the water in the well has never been exhausted nor even in short supply.

The three types of well may illustrate types of Christians. Christians like the shallow well have their sins forgiven but they fall short of becoming overcomers. Their lives are marked by one failure after another. True, they are born again, but they do not grow and remain as infants indefinitely. As a result they are easily carried away by the winds and currents of false teaching.

Christians in the second group have experienced more of God's grace. Not only are their sins forgiven but they have also been delivered from the bondage of sin. They have not only been born again but have also manifested their new life in growth.

But it is only Christians in the third group who can be compared to wells with bubbling springs.

They trust the Lord not only to maintain their own spiritual life but also to impart power for witness and zeal for service. Neither adverse circumstances nor the machinations of men can disturb their peace or joy.

3. Why are there wells without water?

How does a situation arise in which certain wells have no water? Since it is designated a well it must once have contained water. And if it is now without water there must be a reason. Let us consider possible reasons.

First, the well may have been neglected. Perhaps it lost its cover so that dust from the road was continually blown into it. After many days and years the well became silted up. This represents Christians who aspire after the world, as Demas did, or who neglect their spiritual life and fall into sin. They are unwilling to change their ways and thus become wells without water.

Secondly, Christians who try to engage in activities beyond their spiritual intake become like dried-up wells. They are so busy in their service for the Lord that they crowd out time for prayer, and they are not replenished as they should be through fellowship with the Lord.

A third possible reason is action from outside, as when enemies throw stones that block the well and prevent it storing water. The wells dug by Abraham, for instance, were stopped up by the deliberate action of his enemies. Not surprisingly the Lord Jesus pronounced woe on those who caused others to stumble. But, although all Christians have enemies who aim to make them stumble, it is not necessary for us to give way to them. For we have resources in the power of God. We read in Psalm 68:17 that "The chariots of God are tens of thousands and thousands of thousands: the Lord has come from Sinai into his sanctuary." God provides chariots for his children to counter any force that may arise to oppose and attack them. The wise will make use of chariots to travel far and fast, while the stupid continue to lie on the ground where they are trampled under foot. So, many Christians have no resources to meet and counter poverty or tribulation, and they become wells without water.

A fourth possible reason for lack of water is the occurrence of earthquakes. Such an upheaval may cause the waters of the spring to change direction and leave the well to dry up. During recent years in China we have grown accustomed both to natural disasters and to man-made cataclysms. Calamities have arisen due to forces both inside and outside the country. The whole world, in fact, is in a very pitiable state. The effect on some Christians is to make them turn their back on truth, and they become as wells without water.

4. How can the supply of water from a well be maintained?
We come to the fourth and most important question. How can wells without water be restored? The first step is to clear out the rubble. A certain church was at one time strong in faith, and God greatly honoured those who had put their trust in Him. For many years their needs had been supplied and their witness had been blessed by God. But suddenly the situation changed. It was as if the well had become stopped up. Contributions to the church dried up and its glory departed. For lack of spiritual food,

Christians were in danger of starving. Naturally they began to enquire into the situation. It was then discovered that a pastor among them had embezzled public funds, thus defrauding others in order to benefit himself. When he eventually made public confession of his sin and promised to make restitution, the stones that had blocked the well were removed and the flow of living water from the church was resumed. And once again they enjoyed God's blessing.

The second step is to make shallow waters deeper. It is essential that the spiritual life of Christians be one of growth. Their knowledge of God must ever grow deeper. This will result from daily reading of His word, maintaining fellowship with God in prayer, and dealing with God through all the stresses and bitternesses of life. Every step forward in the knowledge of God means a corresponding increase in spiritual power, and also a further distance from the sinful habits of the past. As your conscience becomes enlightened, things that even a year ago never troubled you are now revealed as out of place. Christians must be ever surging forward. Their knowledge of God must ever deepen.

The third step is to see that the wells are well covered and protected from both dust blown in by the wind and stones thrown in by enemies. In an address to the bride in the Song of Songs we read "You are a garden locked up, my sister, my bride; you are a spring enclosed, a sealed fountain" (Song of Sol. 4:12). According to Exodus 21:33 the law of Moses included the following requirement: "If a man uncovers a pit or digs one and fails to cover it and an ox or a donkey falls into it, the owner of the pit must pay for the loss; he must pay its owner and the dead animal will be his." Any man who dug a pit had to cover it. This illustrates a spiritual truth and calls to mind Paul's words to Timothy: "Watch your life and doctrine closely. Persevere in them, because if you do, you will save both yourself and your hearers" (1 Timothy 4:16).

You must at all costs preserve your life of communion with God. Do not give it up! Do not cut it short! No matter how busy you are, you must read your Bible and you must pray every day. Set apart a time to be quiet in the presence of God. Your communion with God is in one sense like a conversation on the telephone. You must not only speak, you must also listen. In speaking with God there is nothing that you may not talk about. But you must never neglect to listen to what God says to you. We must adopt the attitude of Samuel. "Speak, Lord, for your servant is listening" (1 Sam.3:9).

It is in that way that we can protect the well from drying up.

Our Debts

Wilson Wang (Wang zi)

THE LORD JESUS will soon return. When He comes He will judge all believers, and at that time we must all stand before the judgement seat and give an account of ourselves. "You then, why do you judge your brother? Or why do you look down on your brother? For we will all stand before God's judgement seat...So then, each of us will give an account of himself to God" (Rom. 14:10,12). Judgement is also described in the Scriptures as reckoning accounts.

Compare 1 Peter 4:5, "But they will have to give account to him who is ready to judge the living and the dead."

What we fear most of all is that, when we stand before the judgement seat of Christ to render account, our unpaid debts will be uncovered. This means that whenever we contemplate the Lord's return we cannot escape being grieved because of our outstanding debts. In 1 Corinthians 11:31 it is written, "But if we judged ourselves, we would not come under judgement." In accordance with what is written here we are now going to "judge ourselves", so that we can pay our debts before the Lord returns and thus avoid being ashamed at his coming.

As I see it, our debts may be classified in three ways: to God, to believers, and to non-believers.

1. To God — owing glory

Romans 3:23 tells us that "all have sinned and fall short of the glory of God." This verse is frequently quoted with reference to unbelievers. We have acted wickedly and offended God, and we have no deeds that bring Him glory. This was certainly the situation before we turned to the Lord in repentance.

But what is the situation now that we have been redeemed? Ought we not to cast off all our sinful habits, and to be in fear and trembling lest we again fall short of His glory? In 1 Corinthians 6:20 it is written, "You were bought at a price. Therefore honour God with your body." This verse signifies that since we are recipients of God's grace we are also the recipients of a heavy responsibility — the way we act in our bodies has a bearing on the glory of God's name. Alas! On many occasions and in many ways we have fallen short of God's glory.

Matthew 5:16 says, "In the same way, let your light shine before men that they may see your good deeds and praise your Father in heaven." There are numerous occasions, however, when the deeds of believers do not reach the standard of unbelievers. John 15:8 tells us, "This is to my Father's glory, that you bear much fruit, showing yourselves to be my disciples." We may have believed in the Lord some years ago, but have we glorified God in our fruit-bearing? With the blessing of God there are many kinds of fruit we ought to be bearing. For instance, there is "fruit in keeping with repentance" (Matt. 3:8); "the fruit of the Spirit" (Gal. 5:22); "the fruit of the light" (Ephesians 5:9) and so on. All these fruits we ought to be bearing. But have we been bearing them? Further, can it be described as *much* fruit? Psalm 50:23 says, "He who sacrifices thank-offerings honours me." But there are many believers who are full of trouble and complaints from morning till night. Nothing satisfies them and no sound of thanksgiving or praise is heard from them. Where can we find believers who are full of peace and joy? David used to praise the Lord seven times a day. Are there any believers today who do that?

Beloved brothers! Only as we are joyful can we glorify God. For unless we are joyful the people of the world will think that the Lord is treating us harshly, and that our burden is heavy. At the time when the Lord Jesus was leaving the world He said to the Father, "I have brought you glory on earth..." Are we in a position to say the same? I fear we all need to confess that we have all fallen short in bringing glory to God.

2. To believers — owing love

Love is depicted in the Bible as to be valued very highly. 1 Corinthians 12:31 shows it to be among "the greater gifts" and as "the most excellent way". 1 Corinthians 13:13 reveals that among faith, hope and love, love is the greatest. 1 Peter 4:8 tells us that "love covers over a multitude of sins" and in Galatians 5:22 it is listed as the first fruit of the Spirit. From Colossians 3:14 we learn that it binds together all the virtues and 1 Timothy 1:5 speaks of it as "the goal of this command". Love is God's special characteristic (1 John 4:8). Obviously no Christian can be without love. He must strive for it with all his might. So it is no surprise to read in Romans 13:8, "Let no debt remain outstanding, except the continuing debt to love one another."

1 Corinthians 13 is the chapter that deals most fully with love, and we should regard it as a mirror, showing up the places where we are still in debt. Love "does not envy". Are we envious? When we see other peope being blessed by God, do we open our lips to give God praise? When we hear of those who are greatly used by God, are we in our hearts really pleased? Love "is not proud". Those who are not proud are hungry and thirsty for the Lord's teaching and listen to it with joy. Are we like that? Love "keeps no record of wrongs" — whether uttered or practised. Do we recall people's good points or their bad points? If we go through this chapter verse by verse and let it search our hearts through and through, we shall find that in the realm of love we are still greatly in debt.

3. To non-believers — owing the gospel

The apostle Paul wrote to the Romans, "I am already

under obligation (AV 'I am debtor') alike to Greek-speaking races and to others, to cultured and to uncultured people; so that for my part I am willing and eager to proclaim the Good News to you also who are in Rome" (Rom.1:14,15 Weymouth).

Were we to conduct a survey of our country we should realize that innumerable people have still not heard the name of Jesus. On whose shoulders does this responsibility lie? Have the people of our own clan been saved? Our relatives? Our friends and neighbours?

The Lord does not want anyone to perish but everyone to come to repentance. So He committed this ministry of saving people to His disciples. When we consider this commission we have to ask ourselves whether or not we are in debt to the unsaved. When the apostle Paul was bidding farewell to the elders at Ephesus he said, "I declare to you today that I am innocent of the blood of all men. For I have not hesitated to proclaim to you the whole will of God" (Acts 20:26, 27). Are we in a position to say, like the apostle Paul, that we have completely carried out our duty to proclaim the gospel and that the blame for what is left undone cannot be placed on us? Paul wrote to the Romans, "From Jerusalem all the way around to Illyricum, I have fully proclaimed the gospel of Christ...there is no more place for me to work in these regions" (Rom. 15:19,25). Are we in a position to make a similar assertion?

No! Our debts in this connection are too numerous. We are not seeing souls saved as we should be. Who will shoulder this responsibility? In the sight of God what is the value of a single soul? Psalm 49:8 says that "the ransom for a life is costly, no payment is ever enough." Clearly a soul is far more precious than property and possessions. And Matthew 16:26 asks the question, "What good will it be for a man if he gains the whole world, yet forfeits his soul?" Clearly a soul is of more value than all things in the world put together. Peter wrote, "You know that it was not with perishable things such as silver or gold that you were redeemed from the empty way of life handed down to you from your forefathers, but with the precious blood of Christ." And Paul said, "You have been bought with a price." Clearly, the value of a soul is beyond reckoning. So if we are in debt to the amount of only one soul, that is something far greater than 10,000 yuan or 100,000 yuan.

The Lord Jesus once said, "I tell you the truth, you will not get out (i.e. of prison) until you have paid the last penny." Could any word be of greater seriousness than this? And this is what Paul had to say, "When I preach the gospel I cannot boast, for I am compelled to preach. Woe to me if I do not preach the gospel." My prayer is that we may emulate the apostle Paul in more ways than one — to be willing like him to preach the gospel, and to learn what he meant when he said that he was "compelled" to preach the gospel.

These then are our debts — to God, to one another, and to those who have not heard the gospel. Let us be on the watch lest we become like the church at Laodicea and regard ourselves as being rich and needing nothing (Rev. 3:14-18). For it is just when we feel ourselves to be owing nothing that our debts are probably the greatest.

We must guard against feeling superior and self-satisfied, and comparing ourselves with other people. We must compare ourselves with the Lord. In Daniel 5:27 we read, "You have been weighed on the scales and found wanting." When we compare ourselves with the Lord it will bring to light the extent of our debt. All debtors are to be pitied, but those who have debts and who yet remain self-satisfied are to be pitied even more.

May the Lord make us aware of our debts and enable us to pay all our debts. We shall in that way prepare ourselves for the day that is to come, when we shall see Him face to face.

Behold! The Judge is standing at the door!

7 CHALLENGING YOUNG PEOPLE

Pearls of Wisdom
(A Letter To A Young Christian)

Wang Mingdao

THE TIME IS NOW approaching when you will be going away to take up your first position. As you enter a new phase in your life and set out to build a career, I write to assure you that I have great expectations for your future. It is my hope that all those excellent qualities already developed in ordinary circumstances will now become apparent in your future work. We trust that in this way you will influence those around you for good, and in so doing bring glory to God. You are, I know, a highly intelligent person, and I am sure you will ponder what I write.

When you first move to a new location to engage in business, you will soon make your first contacts with new associates. They have not known you before, and inevitably their first impressions of you will remain for a long time. These may be of such a nature that after a while you would like to change or modify them, but you will not find it easy to do so. But if these early impressions reflect your good character you will find it easier to win esteem and love. Even if later on people become aware of your shortcomings they will tend to overlook them. On the other hand, if their first impressions of you are bad they will soon resent your attitude and begin to dislike you. And even though they later observe some of your good points they will not easily get rid of the earlier unfavourable impressions.

As you settle in, therefore, you must be one hundred per cent careful in your words, conduct and habits. You must avoid unnecessarily annoying people and causing them to look down on you. It is vitally important that you show yourself to be a person who can be trusted. To lose credibility is to become devalued. You have to build up the quality of reliability in the same way that you build a house. You must first assemble all the necessary material and then add to it many months of labour. Only then will a house materialize. However, suppose you are careless for a moment, when the house is finished, and unthinkingly throw away a lighted match. The entire building can be destroyed within an hour, and the result of many months of hard work will in no time become a heap of ashes. It is the same with your life. So in all things be sincere, in your words, actions and heart.

Always carry out your duties faithfully, whether they are small or large. Do not lightly make promises, but once you have made a promise be sure you carry it out. Don't appropriate anything that doesn't belong to you. Be absolutely honest with all the money that passes through your hands. When you give an undertaking to do something for somebody, do it with all your strength. Do not lightly lend money to anyone, and do not resort to borrowing. But if you should need to borrow money, then make a point of paying it back at the earliest opportunity. Never take advantage of people. When you make an appointment, see to it that you arrive in time. Do not pass on information which you are not sure is accurate. Avoid exaggeration! In business affairs be ready to shoulder responsibilty. When you discover you have made a mistake, confess it frankly.

All these things are necessary to build up a reputation for credibility and reliability. And remember, even when you have built it up, you still need to preserve it. It only needs one untrue word, dishonest action or insincere business dealing, and your good reputation may be destroyed overnight.

When you first arrive to take up your new post, do not be afraid to acknowledge that you are a follower of the Lord Jesus. It may be that, as a result, people will look down on you and even insult you. In such a situation do not forget that the Lord Jesus, in order to be your Saviour, was reviled and persecuted beyond all other men. He was arrested, beaten, humiliated, and finally nailed to a cross of wood. It was for you that He endured all this shame and suffering. It is the measure of His love for you. How can you do anything but confess Him before men?

You must acknowledge that you are a follower of the Lord Jesus Christ at the first opportunity. To do it later is much more difficult. The longer you wait the harder it will become. It is certainly hard going, like negotiating a narrow pass through the mountains, to acknowledge the Lordship of Christ in the midst of hostile unbelievers. But once you have forced your way through this grim experience you will find that the way ahead becomes progressively easier.

It may be that those who have dedicated their lives to evil will do their best to entice you to drink wine, smoke opium, gamble, conspire with them to acquire property dishonestly, or have illicit relations with one of the other sex. You should tell them frankly that since you are a Christian you do not take part in these things. For if you sturdily reject their advances in this way they will probably make no further effort to embroil you. But if you resort to specious excuses, such as saying that you have no time, you are simply opening a route by which they can put pressure on you again later. And eventually you may weaken and follow them. I am not here giving rein to wild imagination. With my own eyes I have seen this happen to many fine Christian believers. Through fear of giving offence they have begun to weaken, and have ended up by falling into sin.

Whatever your duties, you should endeavour with all your mind and strength to carry them out satisfactorily. Whether seen or unseen, you should be faithful and diligent. Always bear in mind that your Master is always observing you, and He will detect whether or not you are diligent and faithful. Your associates may be lazy and may steal your employers' time. You should not be led astray by this, but should continue diligent and faithful. For you are also the servant of Christ.

Sooner or later you are bound to meet obstacles and difficulties. It is your task to learn to overcome them. Who has ever faced greater difficulties than our Lord? Yet He was never disheartened. "He will not falter or be discouraged till he establishes justice on earth" (Isa. 42:4), It was when Jesus was praying in the Garden of Gethsemane that He encountered the greatest difficulty of all. Yet He was able to say

"My Father, if it is not possible for this cup to be taken away unless I drink it, may your will be done" (Matt. 26:42). He did not evade His cross and as a consequence He received the crown of glory and honour. So it is with us. Only as we refuse to side-step the cross shall we qualify to receive the crown that God has prepared for us. So don't be put off by difficulties.

You will meet people who are considerably wealthier than you are. Do not envy them or covet their possessions. In handling of property and possessions, be one hundred per cent clear, sincere and careful. Do not use public property for your own private purposes. Even though other people take liberties of this kind, be sure that you yourself are not contaminated. You may find yourself without surplus money in your hand, restricted to the plainest food, and with only old clothes to wear, but so long as you have a conscience void of offence towards both God and man, this is far better than enjoying dishonourably-acquired affluence.

Do not assume an attitude of superiority towards those with whom you share accommodation. Pride is the pathway to shame. It may be true that you have some outstanding good points, but do not overlook the fact that you also have shortcomings, and other people also have good points. Being aware of your own shortcomings will keep you from pride, and bearing in mind others' good points will keep you from looking down on them. Proud people provoke resentment. Arrogant people will sooner or later lose their place in society. If a person who is virtuous can also be humble he is like a king who wears a crown inlaid with precious stones. Never let down your guard against becoming proud.

Do not be envious of those who enjoy greater

success than you do. "A heart at peace gives life to the body, but envy rots the bones" (Prov. 14:30).

Always bear in mind that your objective in doing business is not to become wealthy, not to amass property, not to enjoy happiness or receive honour. Your objective is to glorify God, to serve your fellow men, and faithfully to carry out the duties that God has entrusted to you.

Every morning, before you plunge into the business of the day, you ought to wait on God for guidance, and seek His instruction, protection and provision. When you are in difficulty or meet temptation you need God to direct and help you. Keep in mind the Scripture, "Trust in the Lord with all your heart and lean not on your own understanding; in all your ways acknowledge him, and he will make your paths straight" (Prov. 3:5,6).

May the hand of God be on you continually — guiding you, keeping you, and sustaining you. May He make His grace and His truth abound towards you. And may He enable you every day to press ahead!

8 ENCOURAGING THE DOWNHEARTED AND TROUBLED

Don't be discouraged!

Wang Mingdao

"He will not falter or be discouraged till he establishes justice on earth" (Isa. 42:4).

Is some source of suffering in your life exactly like Paul's thorn in the flesh? Although you have asked the Lord repeatedly to take it away, He has never granted your request. Don't be discouraged. If the Lord has not yet removed your physical handicap it is so that His power may be made manifest in you. So never forget His words of assurance: "My grace is sufficient for you, for my power is made perfect in weakness" (2 Cor. 12:9).

Or perhaps you are passing through a period of testing, and even after many days you have still not been released from this trial. Don't be discouraged! Remember that the Lord wants to refine those who belong to Him as silver and gold are refined. "'See, I will send my messenger, who will prepare the way before me. Then suddenly the Lord you are seeking will come to his temple; the messenger of the covenant, whom you desire, will come,' says the Lord Almighty. But who can endure the day of his coming? Who can stand when he appears? For he will be like a refiner's fire or a launderer's soap. He will sit as a refiner and purifier of silver; he will purify the Levites and refine them like gold and silver..." (Malachi 3:1-3).

When silver and gold are refined it is necessary for them not only to be submitted to the fierce heat of the fire, but also to be kept there for an extended period. The longer the period of exposure to the heat the purer they become. If God allows you to spend many days in the fire of testing, it is so that all the blemishes may be removed and you may be purified as metal is purified.

If you are faithful in the work you do for God, and if you do battle in the cause of God's truth, you may yourself be threatened, attacked and persecuted by wicked men. Are you on this account losing heart? Is your purpose weakened? Don't be discouraged! The apostle Paul had experiences like this, but the Lord spoke to him in a vision and said, "Do not be afraid; keep on speaking, do not be silent. For I am with you, and no one is going to attack and harm you, because I have many people in this city" (Acts 18:9,10). The One who promised to be with Paul will certainly be with you also. The One who protected Paul then will certainly protect you today.

It may be that the trials and misfortunes you encounter seem too heavy for you, and you fear you will be crushed by them. Don't be discouraged! Remember the promise of God! "When you pass through the waters, I will be with you; and when you pass through the rivers, they will not sweep over you. When you walk through the fire, you will not be burned; the flames will not set you ablaze" (Isa. 43:2). Again — "No temptation has seized you except what is common to man. And God is faithful; he will not let you be tempted beyond what you can bear. But when you are tempted, he will also provide a way out so that you can stand up under it" (1 Cor. 10:13).

Although your conduct is upright and free from blame, you may be reviled and falsely accused because you follow Christ and seek to do God's will. Do you feel very bitter about this? Don't be discouraged! Remember the promise of the Lord Jesus, "Blessed are those who are persecuted because of righteousness, for theirs is the kingdom of heaven. Blessed are you when people insult you, persecute you and falsely say all kinds of evil against you because of me. Rejoice and be glad, because great is your reward in heaven, for in the same way they persecuted the prophets who were before you" (Matt. 5:11,12).

It may be that having been sent by God to minister to certain people, you soon discover that they are totally unresponsive and stubborn. They have no intention whatever of receiving the message you are preaching to them. Does such an experience dishearten you? Don't be discouraged! There was a prophet who encountered a situation like this. But God said to him, "And you, son of man, do not be afraid of them or their words. Do not be afraid, though briers and thorns are all around you and you live among scorpions. Do not be afraid of what they say or terrified by them, though they are a rebellious house. You must speak my words to them, whether they listen or fail to listen, for they are rebellious" (Ezek. 2:6,7). God also said, "But I will make you as unyielding and hardened as they are. I will make your forehead like the hardest stone, harder than flint. Do not be afraid of them or terrified by them, though they are a rebellious house" (Ezek. 3:8,9).

All your dealings with people may be loving and you may always exert yourself to help them, but in spite of this they not only ignore the favour you show them but even become your enemies. Are you therefore disheartened, and tempted to abandon your desire to do good? Don't be discouraged! Remember the Lord Jesus! He loved us so greatly that He was willing to renounce the glory of heaven and become a man. Throughout His life He endured all kinds of bitter suffering, and finally did not hesitate to give His life in order to redeem us. But people not only ignored the grace He had shown towards them, but even hated and persecuted Him and put Him to death. This is the attitude that has prevailed all down the years. Yet the Lord has always had compassion on men and been patient towards them, always hoping that men would repent. In all these things He is our example; how can we who are His disciples do other than follow it?

It may be that you see evil men flourishing while the upright are insulted and trampled on. Do you therefore grow disheartened and conclude that you need no longer strive to maintain your integrity? I urge you, don't be discouraged! Listen to what God has to say. "Do not fret because of evil men or be envious of those who do wrong; for like the grass they will soon wither, like green plants they will soon die away. Trust in the Lord and do good; dwell in the land and enjoy safe pasture. Delight yourself in the Lord and he will give you the desire of your heart. Commit your way to the Lord; trust in him and he will do this: He will make your righteousness shine like the dawn, the justice of your cause like the noonday sun. Be still before the Lord and wait patiently for him; do not fret when men succeed in their ways, when they carry out their wicked schemes" (Psalm 37:1-7).

It may be that for many days you pray earnestly about some particular matter. You are convinced it is according to the will of God. But even after a long time you have still not received what you prayed for. Do you on this account lose heart? I urge you, don't be discouraged! Remember what the Lord Jesus had to say about the friend who came seeking bread at midnight (Luke 11:5-13). The one who eventually agreed to give bread did not do so because he was a friend, but because of the caller's persistence.

Remember also the parable in which the widow petitioned the unrighteous judge to grant her justice against her adversary (see Luke 18:1-8). The unrighteous judge was moved to act not because he loved the widow but simply to stop her bothering him. Our heavenly Father, on the other hand, loves us beyond all description. How much more will he listen, in the end, to our petitions!

It may be you are deeply conscious that the world is daily becoming more depraved and the power of darkness is daily increasing. Does this lead you to the conclusion that God's plan to save the world is a complete failure? I urge you, don't be discouraged! You should be aware that the deeper the darkness the nearer is the daybreak. The depravity of the world does not signify that God's plan is a failure, but that His purposes will soon be fulfilled. For the Bible tells us that at a time when evil and depravity are intensified the king of peace and justice will suddenly descend to welcome His disciples and, at the same time, to set in motion the judgement of the world. He will then set up His kingdom of justice and peace.

It may be that you have observed other Christians' abundant gifts and opportunities compared with your own, and taken note of the widespread nature of their work. You are conscious that you are not so richly endowed with gifts, do not have such good opportunities and cannot show the same abundant results. So you are disappointed and depressed. But I beg you not to be discouraged. What God requires of us is not success but rather faithfulness.

Has anyone ever been placed in a situation more grievous than that in which our Lord Jesus Christ was placed? Has anyone ever had to endure greater trials than those faced by the Lord Jesus? Has anyone ever had experiences more calculated to make one lose heart than those of the Lord Jesus? Yet in spite of all He was never discouraged nor did He ever give up hope in His quest to establish justice on earth.

I speak to you who are followers of the Lord Jesus Christ. No matter what discouraging circumstances and trials and hardships you meet, on no account allow yourself to lose heart. Always keep in view the example of Christ Himself. And never be discouraged!

Faithful to the point of death
(Revelation 2:8-11)

David Yang

SUFFERING MARKS the pathway of the Cross. It was by travelling this road that the Lord and all His faithful followers entered into the glory of God. So it was with Paul and the prophets and saints of old. Unremittingly down the years the footmarks of those who entered into glory are stained with blood.

The Lord exhorted the messenger of the church at Smyrna: "Be faithful, even to the point of death, and I will give you the crown of life." But believers today quickly become alarmed at the thought of difficulty. Let persecution raise its head and they will hurriedly pull back. They think only of peace and rest as the blessing of God, entirely forgetting His reminder: "In the world you have tribulation, but take courage, I have overcome the world" (John 16:33). The Lord never deceived His followers by promising only the material blessings of salvation. His warning could not be clearer: "They will lay their hands on you and will persecute you" (Luke 21:12).

I know your afflictions and your poverty
The church at Smyrna was truly suffering tribulation for the Lord. Satan had caused several believers to be thrown into prison. Other saints were facing mockery, threats, cursing and persecution. Yet they remained unflinchingly loyal to their Lord. From church history we learn that the suffering of this church continued and that it was Smyrna which witnessed the martyrdom of Polycarp, a disciple of John, when he was more than eighty years old.

From the viewpoint of the world martyrdom is a

terrifying experience, but the people of God have been shown clearly that this is what to expect: "If you were of the world, the world would love its own; but because you are not of the world, but I chose you out of the world, therefore the world hates you" (John 15:19). It is strange indeed if any Christian is never once called on to face mocking or affliction or persecution on account of his allegiance to Christ. In fact this is a situation which should never exist. It would suggest that he is compromising with sin and engulfed by the world. A true Christian who neither seeks the will of God nor follows in the path of the Lord will encounter but little suffering for his faith. If he suffers at all, it is no more than comes to ordinary people of the world who are naturally subject to sickness and death. This is what is known as misfortune, and is something entirely different from the tribulation referred to in these passages. It is those who suffer hardship for following Christ who are designated victors and gain the Lord's reward.

It is strange perhaps that the Lord did not say to the poor at Smyrna, "I will satisfy your needs;" what He said was: "I know your poverty." But how understanding and wise and moving are these words of the Lord, "I know!" They penetrate right to the heart of those who are His faithful followers. What strength they impart! How satisfying they are! He knows. Our hearts may be at rest.

How often we ask the Lord to remove tribulation and give us prosperity! And indeed we frequently experience such blessing. We are delivered from affliction; we are given riches in place of poverty; and in the presence of our enemies God spreads a table for us. But sometimes the poverty remains and the affliction grows worse. Then the Lord says: "I know."

How simple it would be for the Lord to deliver us from poverty and make us rich. His heart is so full of compassion that He can have no pleasure in the suffering of His children. But in order that we should grow spiritually, become more mature in our experience, be undisputed overcomers, He sometimes withholds deliverance. He enables us to endure to the end so that we may receive the crown of glory. He knows the limits of our strength, and as a Refiner He knows the strength of the fire. Immediately the work is done, without leaving us one second longer, He will remove His beloved child from the hostile furnace. The faith that is tested by fire will be more precious than refined gold.

But you are rich

Too many Christians today are seeking the wealth of the world, and are not prepared to seek the treasures of Heaven. They have faith to be saved but are unwilling to be poor for the sake of Christ. For them, comfort and riches indicate the grace of God. They are ignorant of what Paul wrote about our suffering with Christ and becoming like Him in His death. All they seem to know is that "money answers everything" (Eccles. 10:19); they are ignorant when it comes to the love of God — its length and breadth and depth and height (Eph. 3:18). Yet spiritual riches like faith, trust, joy, strength, patience and many other virtues are all born of poverty.

The slander of the Jews

Tribulation and poverty are sufficiently hard to endure in themselves. But to these is added slander. It was not even the slander of those who do not know God, which can be endured, for they are travelling a different road. But the Jews were supposed to know the things of God. They were the people of God, representative of the Christians of today. How hard it is to endure derision and slander from our fellow Christians! As the Bible says: "A man's enemies will be the members of his household" (Matt. 10:36).

Cast into prison

Imprisonment meant indescribable suffering — a small, dark, filthy cell and a putrid atmosphere. But the Lord exhorted His people not to fear. One source of comfort was that only some believers, not the whole church, would be involved. The few were chosen that through suffering they might bring glory to God and blessing to the church. God therefore permitted Satan to cast some of their number into prison. Apart from them, Satan had no power to touch a single one. "Are not two sparrows sold for a penny? Yet not one of them will fall to the ground apart from the will of your Father ...the very hairs of your head are all numbered" (Matt. 10:29-30). Satan has no power to go beyond the will of God. When God ordained that some of the saints at Smyrna should be cast into prison, Satan could only attack that number, and no more.

To test you

"Refining" immediately suggests precious metals like silver and gold in the hands of a craftsman. A craftsman designs a vessel, and only after proper planning does he put it in the fire. Purpose, planning, method — all are present. As the apostle Peter wrote: "That your faith, — of greater worth than gold, which perishes even though refined by fire — may be proved genuine and may result in praise, glory and honour when Jesus Christ is revealed" (1 Peter 1:7). To recognize this is to banish fear. Even should we be among those whom God selects to suffer imprisonment, words like this ensure our happiness and joy. For affliction is simply the fire which God is using to refine us, that we may become perfect and complete, without blemish. The furnace does not destroy the precious metal but purifies it, raises its value, and makes it glorious. When God places His children in the furnace He is not acting haphazardly, careless of the effect for good or bad, but He is acting with care and purpose. Thus James exhorts us: "Consider it pure joy, my brothers, when you face trials of many kinds" (James 1:2). Just as the craftsman cannot use unrefined metals, so God cannot use untested saints. History is full of men used by God — and all were shaped and moulded in the refining fire of trial.

You will suffer persecution for ten days

The saints must suffer tribulation, and Satan will cast some into prison. But for our encouragement we read that the duration of their suffering is defined; it is kept within certain limits. Not only does God set a limit on the number of those who suffer, but also on the time. One day less would be insufficient; one day more is impossible. When God determines ten days, that is what He means. No one can keep them in prison for twelve days, or even eleven, when God says ten. The prolongation of imprisonment even for one second is unthinkable. Praise God! He is still King of kings and Lord of lords and His throne is established in Heaven. His authority extends everywhere. Nothing in the universe is outside the range of His omnipotent commands. With God's permission, Satan may be as fierce as a lion, but he has no authority to go beyond what God permits. Consider Job. God took Job's possessions and put them in the hands of Satan. But Satan could not touch Job's body for God had forbidden him, saying, "On the man himself do not lay a finger," (Job 1:12).

Christian! In view of the afflictions, poverty and slander, are you not inclined to be fearful? Tribulation abounds; the days of poverty stretch out; and you are left with only a little wheat and oil. But let your heart be at rest. Our merciful heavenly Father is only testing us to make us pure and precious and usable. He knows exactly what burdens are more than we can bear and will not require us to bear them. God is faithful, and when we are tested will certainly open a way of escape that we may be able to bear it (1 Cor. 10:13).

Be faithful, even to the point of death

The worst that Satan can do is to cause death. Beyond death he has no power or authority whatsoever. Neither his poisoned hooks, his claws, nor his fiery darts can affect us beyond death. So the things he inflicts in this life — tribulation, poverty, slander, imprisonment — are all terminated at death. That is why the Lord exhorts His Church to be faithful to death. We may not necessarily be brought to that extremity, but if we are ready to die for the Lord then there is nothing that Satan can do to harm us.

Christian, what is your attitude to death? Is it something to be feared? For those without hope it is, because the second death and judgement await them. But for the children of God, death is the gateway to glory. If it means meeting the Lord Jesus face to face, how glad we should be to reach the other side! If God wills that we should depart from our bed, amid the songs of the saints, that is a happy death. But if we die on the battlefield in conflict with Satan, that is a glorious death indeed.

Even though death itself is not involved we should regard a steadfast *willingness* to die for the Lord as a weapon with which to resist all kinds of evil — the lust of the flesh and the attacks of Satan. As Peter said: "Therefore, since Christ suffered in his body, arm yourselves also with the same attitude, because he who has suffered in his body is done with sin. As a result he does not live the rest of his earthly life for evil human desires, but rather for the will of God" (1 Pet. 4:1,2).

The things we lust for are the things which indulge the flesh: gossip, criticism, frivolous talk, giving rein to pleasure. But to indulge the flesh is to invoke untold spiritual loss. On the contrary, if we are ready to suffer in the flesh, then when we are tempted to criticize, envy or hate people, we can immediately say to ourselves: "The Lord has died for me; I am no longer my own and I no longer seek my own pleasure." This is to be more than conqueror.

I will give you the crown of life

A crown is a reward for the victor. It is prepared for those who for the Lord's sake have endured tribulation, suffering, imprisonment, poverty, slander and derision, and have remained faithful even unto death. If we anticipate glory in the future, we must achieve glory now. If we hope to reign in the future, we must learn to reign now. God's gifts are given so that we may be like Christ. Thus He not only gives us things to enjoy, but also ordains affliction. Christ, even though God's Son, learned obedience by what He suffered (Heb. 5:8). To share in His glory, we must also tread the same pathway.

Blessed are those who are persecuted because of righteousness

Wang Mingdao
(1 Peter 4:12–16, Revelation 2:10)

BLESSED ARE THOSE who are persecuted because of righteousness, for theirs is the kingdom of heaven. Blessed are you when people insult you, persecute you and falsely say all kinds of evil against you because of me. Rejoice and be glad, because great is your reward in heaven, for in the same way they persecuted the prophets who were before you. (Matthew 5: 10-12)

It is easy, when reading this passage of Scripture, to think of it as simply refering to the persecution of believers in New Testament times. But when we study the history of the church we find that, whenever the gospel is first preached in a particular area, preachers and believers are almost invariably subject to opposition and attack. The lighter forms of persecution would consist of mocking and cursing, and in times of severe persecution preachers would be beaten, thrown into prison, or even put to death.

This was the situation when the gospel was first preached in East Asia. And when the gospel was first preached in western Europe it was the same. From the first century to the third, many Christians encountered severe persecution and were cruelly put to death because of their allegiance to Christ. Some were put to death with the sword; some were crucified; some were burnt to death; and some were thrown into the arena with wild beasts.

In the light of the Lord's promise in the verses quoted above we can rejoice to know that all these suffering Christians can be described as "blessed". For what they endured was "because of righteousness". And when the glory of Christ is revealed they will receive their reward and be glorified with Him.

Perhaps we are disappointed that we do not qualify for such a reward. And yet, are we right in this assumption? Is it only those referred to above who enjoy this promised blessedness? Are we of the present generation denied the opportunity to suffer for righteousness? Whenever a person genuinely believes in the Lord, loving Him sincerely and serving Him faithfully, before long he or she is cursed and attacked and persecuted. This was the situation in days of old, and is still so today. For in a world where Satan wields authority it is impossible for those who truly love the Lord to avoid persecution.

We may recall what the Lord said to His disciples: "If the world hates you, keep in mind that it hated me first. If you belonged to the world, it would love you as its own. As it is, you do not belong to the world, but I have chosen you out of the world. That is why the world hates you. Remember the words I spoke to you: 'No servant is greater than his master.' If they persecuted me, they will persecute you also. If they obeyed my teaching, they will obey yours also" (John 15:18-21). One thing is clear: if we really belong to Christ, it will be quite impossible for us to escape persecution at the hands of the world.

First reason for persecution: what we believe is not what they believe.
We believe in God and in the Bible; we believe that

God's warnings and promises are to be taken seriously; we believe that Jesus Christ was crucified for our sin, rose from among the dead and one day will come again to receive us to Himself and we shall ever be with the Lord. We believe further that God will execute judgement on this world of evil and set up His kingdom.

The truths that we accept are regarded by those who worship idols as heresy, while atheists and materialists regard them as superstitions. We know that our faith is neither heresy nor superstition, and that the facts of our faith are incontrovertible. But alas! The god of this world has blinded men's eyes so that everything is turned upside down and black and white are reversed. "They describe evil as good and good as evil; they regard darkness as light and light as darkness; they regard sweetness as bitterness and bitterness as sweetness." So those who truly believe in Christ, on account of their faith will be reviled and opposed and persecuted by the world. The stronger a believer's faith the fiercer the opposition.

Second reason: we are intent on doing the will of God and on pleasing Him while "the whole world is under the control of the evil one" who is God's enemy (1 John 5:19).

It is quite logical for those who belong to the world to have their place in the evil one's programme. The inevitable consequence, therefore, is that those who belong to the world and those who belong to Christ will everywhere be in conflict. The tendency of those who belong to Satan is to speak vainly and deceitfully, while the tendency of those who belong to Christ is to speak sincerely and uprightly. Those who belong to Satan worship wealth while those who belong to Christ worship God with all their heart. Those who belong to Satan take over man-made ideas, including their own, as their standards, while those who belong to Christ take the will of God as revealed in the Scriptures as their standard. Those who belong to Satan tend to seek personal gain at the expense of others, while those who belong to Christ are concerned to promote the interests of others.

In short, those who belong to Satan and those who belong to Christ are not only completely different but inevitably hostile to each other. How can the followers of Satan tolerate those who follow Christ? The followers of Satan regard those who follow Christ as "thorns in the eye", and as such a force to be eliminated.

Third reason: our light shines out in the darkness.
The deeds of those who love the world are crooked, and those who do them hate the light that shows them up. The Bible tells us, with reference to the coming of the Lord, that "the light shines in the darkness, but the darkness has not overcome it" (John 1:5). The Bible also tells us that "light has come into the world, but men loved darkness instead of light because their deeds were evil. Everyone who does evil hates the light, and will not come into the light for fear that his deeds will be exposed" (John 3:19, 20).

The Lord Jesus declared that He was the light of the world (John 8:12). He also expected those who belong to Him to be the light of the world (Matt. 5:14). Whenever all the members of a particular group are wicked there is nothing to show up the destable nature of what they do, and nothing disturbs their equanimity. But if a follower of Christ comes into their midst the sanctified life he lives will immediately expose the evil nature of their deeds. If the evil-doers, as a result, become grieved over their sin and return to the light, there is no problem. But alas! Only a small proportion of them are prepared to act in this way. Most, far from reproving themselves, only condemn the Christians for causing them embarrassment by showing up their faults. They become angry, and vent their anger in reviling and persecuting the Christians.

Fourth reason: Christians' manner of life is beyond the world's comprehension.

As a result of believing in Christ there is a new dimension in their lives. Their spiritual eyes are opened to see the God who loves them and the Lord who redeemed them. They have a vision of the eternal home that the Lord has prepared for them, and they are enriched by all His wonderful promises. This means that their whole manner of life is different from that of unbelievers. Since those who belong to the world have no faith, then all these spiritual benefits are hidden from their view. All that they observe is that Christian believers are different. They do not understand them, and out of misunderstanding arises hostility and persecution. Christian believers love their Lord and want to turn their back on sinful habits and be faithful servants of the Lord. But this is totally beyond the comprehension of unbelievers, who fiercely accuse them of pretending to be good while at the same time having ulterior motives.

Christians are unwilling to adopt the malpractices common around them. They love their fellow men and desire to share with them the benefits of the gospel. They therefore seek to lead them to the Lord. But all this is beyond the comprehension of unbelievers, who insist that these activities are dictated solely with a view to personal profit.

Fifty years ago Chinese people accused missionaries of poisoning wells, kidnapping people and even gouging out their eyes. In recent years they have designated Chinese preachers as "running dogs" of imperialistic foreigners and pioneers in cultural aggression. Misunderstanding leads to persecution and this means that the Christian's every step is fraught with danger.

Fifth reason: Christians must point out the sins of others.

Our Lord once said to his brothers: "The world cannot hate you, but it hates me because I testify that what it does is evil" (John 7:7). Those who truly belong to Christ are bound to imitate Him, and to follow His example. Among the practices of Christ is that of testifying to people's sin. When Christians adopt this practice it is certainly not in order to vent their anger to ruin people's reputations, or to deny them their advantages and benefits. Their purpose is to help people to repent and to turn their back on their sins, and thus to lead them to a saving knowledge of Christ. However, in order to lead people to repentance it is necessary first to make them aware of their sin. They must be warned of the danger that lies ahead if they do not repent. So Christians must testify that the practices of the world are evil. But the world cannot tolerate this. By nature men and women want to receive commendation and be eulogized. They are unwilling to listen to unpleasant truths which, though faithfully presented, grate on the ear. Far from flattering the world, faithful Christians can only point out that its deeds are evil. No wonder they are met with hatred, anger and persecution.

Once we grasp the reasons for persecution we shall understand that, unless those to whom Christians address themselves repent, the persecution of Christians is inevitable. So long as Satan holds power in the world, so long will Christians have to endure persecution. For until the day that Christ returns to deal with Satan (Rev. 20:1-3), the devil will continue to exercise authority in the world. We cannot avoid the conclusion, therefore, that this evil generation will continue to engineer the persecution of Christian believers.

Some will be persecuted by neighbours and relatives. Some will be mocked and despised, reviled and blasphemed. Some will encounter hatred and hostility. Some will be subject to assault and physical injury. Some will be put to death. The Bible clearly tells us that "everyone who wants to live a godly life in Christ Jesus will be persecuted" (2 Tim. 3:12). The facts tells us clearly that this description is absolutely accurate.

The Christian is therefore faced with two possible kinds of persecution. One is being put to death, the other is facing continual insults and assaults. Which do you think is the more difficult? Which is of greater value? We would almost certainly reply that those who lay down their lives for Christ will receive the greater reward. However, when you ponder the matter, you realize that to endure the insults and assaults of the world daily, yet never turn aside, compromise with sin or go hand in hand with the world — and all this because of love for Christ — this is no easier or of less value than laying down one's life for Him.

In fact, it can be said that to maintain one's faith

while enduring insults and suffering persecution for a prolonged period is more difficult than standing for the truth by laying down one's life. In order to achieve the latter it is only necessary to be strong and courageous for one day. But to endure ridicule, hostility, and persecution continually, without slackening in one's quest, compromising with sin or giving in to the world, even though it goes on for months or years or even tens of years — to reproduce the strength and courage of one day throughout all those days, and all this for the sake of the Lord — that requires even greater faith and courage, and an even higher level of obedience. Surely this is greater victory. And one who overcomes in this way can expect a commensurate reward. This has been promised by the Lord Jesus. "Blessed are you when people insult you, persecute you and falsely say all kinds of evil against you because of me. Rejoice and be glad, because great is your reward in heaven, for in the same way they persecuted the prophets who were before you."

We are accustomed to admiring the saints who have shed their blood for the name of the Lord, and perhaps we covet the kind of reward that is promised to them. We cannot all be martyrs and lay down our lives for the Truth, and we do not at this present time face the kind of persecution that was inflicted on the early Christians by Imperial Rome. Yet we may all engage in meritorious active service as those saints did and we can expect to receive a similar reward. "If we died with him, we will also live with him; if we endure, we will also reign with him" (2 Tim. 2:11).

At this point another question arises. We have seen that a Christian, so long as he is in the world, has no prospect of avoiding persecution. That being so, why are there so many Christians who seem not to suffer even the slightest persecution? Indeed, some are extremely popular and widely respected. The Bible tells us that "everyone who wants to live a godly life in Christ Jesus will be persecuted". It follows therefore that if there are individuals professing to be Christians who are never in any way persecuted by the world, it must be because they actually belong to the world and not to Christ. "They are from the world and therefore speak from the viewpoint of the world, and the world listens to them" (1 John 4:5).

Many people who call themselves Christians are no different, apart from their use of the designation "Christian", from people who belong to the world. They do not believe the foundational truths of the Bible. When they talk about Jesus it is invariably about His character, His virtues, His spirit, His love, and His teaching — but no more. Since they lack the element of faith they do not provoke the mockery and the hostility of the world. The world does not describe them as being superstitious since they have no belief in the unseen. On the contrary, it regards them as ideal Christians. The path they follow is essentially the same as the world's. Further, they are not concerned to do the will of God; it is the world that they seek to please and to imitate. Their tastes for the most part are the tastes of the world. They are not worried about giving offence to God; all that concerns them is to avoid giving offence to people.

Since they tread the same path as the world, the world naturally treats them as its close friends with a common purpose. Because they follow the ways of the world they have no distinctive light to shed in the darkness of the world. Since they share the same characteristics as the world, the question of the world misunderstanding them does not arise. As for drawing attention to sins in the world, it is obvious that they lack the qualifications for such a ministry.

It is nothing short of a calamity that people who do not possess the basic qualification of belonging to Christ should have so much say in the affairs of the church. They are nothing other than the agents of Satan, his undercover forces to attack the church from within. Without the existence of such forces Christians would only need to take precautions against attacks from outside.

So those who belong to Christ must face persecution instigated, on the one hand, by avowed unbelievers and, on the other hand, by counterfeit believers who have somehow insinuated themselves into the ranks of church members. Although these counterfeit believers call themselves Christians they are actually under the control of the one who also masterminds unbelievers, namely Satan.

Such a situation is sad beyond words. For those who belong to Christ fully expect to be ridiculed, derided, reviled, assailed and persecuted on account of their faith by those who do not believe. But counterfeit believers are not called on to suffer such hostility. For they are numbered with unbelievers and the world not only welcomes them into their ranks but actively seeks their co-operation.

Naturally there are also genuine Christians who escape persecution. They may be weak and experience defeat, but they are certainly true believers. In their heart of hearts they have a desire to do the will of God and witness for Him. But they are apprehensive of provoking insults and persecution, so they tend to keep their faith out of sight. Inevitably they forfeit the joy, peace and power which is their birthright. Furthermore, if in this life they sidestep the cross they will in the world to come be denied the crown.

Beloved Christian friends! In dependence on the mighty power of God let us be faithful and courageous warriors of Jesus Christ who is our Lord. Let us not refrain from doing our duty simply because our environment is evil. We are well able to endure the combined attacks of unbelievers on the one hand and counterfeit believers on the other hand, and to remain victors on the field. Whatever the cost let us hold fast the truth and do the will of God to the end. Let us turn away from the blandishments of the evil one. For no matter what losses we incur and no matter how men revile us, we must never give way and never give up. To be firm and unyielding in the face of such pressures requires great determination and courage. But it is the secret of overcoming. And it is only Christians who overcome in this way who can expect to inherit the glorious crown that Christ has promised.

9 WITNESSING TO GOD'S GRACE

A Partner In Marriage

Timothy Dzao
(Zhao Shiguang)

"DO NOT BE YOKED together with unbelievers. For what do righteousness and wickedness have in common? Or what fellowship can light have with darkness? What harmony is there between Christ and Belial? What does a believer have in common with an unbeliever? What agreement is there between the temple of God and idols? For we are the temple of the living God..." Therefore come out from them and be separate' says the Lord" (2 Cor. 6:14-17).

In this letter to the church at Corinth Paul exhorts the believers not to be yoked with unbelievers because we are the temple of the living God.

The Scriptures also tell us that "He who has the Son has life; he who does not have the Son of God does not have life" (1 John 5:12). We learn from this verse that those of us who believe in the Lord are people possessing life, and those who do not believe in the Lord do not possess life. Obviously a living person cannot live with one who is dead.

Marriage is an institution that God highly esteems. This is plain from the words of Jesus: "A man will leave his father and mother and be united to his wife, and the two' will become one flesh" (Mark 10:7,8).

I learned from the above passage of Scripture that I as a servant of the Lord must on no account marry an unbeliever, for this would be displeasing to the Lord. If I did so I should be breaking a rule laid down by the Lord and I would forfeit His blessing.

But my acceptance of this rule was challenged. One evening my mother spoke to me out of the blue on the question of marriage. She said to me in a low voice, and very gravely, "I have found a girl for you. I commissioned relatives to make enquiries on your behalf and I have already spent seven years working on this matter. I have now been successful in finding a wife for you. All that is necessary now is for you to indicate your acceptance of the arrrangement and the whole matter can be brought to a head."

My mother truly loved me, and was also a most compassionate woman. Her proposition created a problem partly because there were many matters that she did not understand and partly because some of her ideas were superstitious and inappropriate. So her opinions were sometimes very different from mine. For example she made use of the horoscope, so when two persons were to be betrothed it was necessary to enquire as to the year, month, day and hour of their birth. According to what she found in my horoscope, it would be best for me to be matched with a woman born in the year of the rat.

On one occasion she apparently remarked to some people rather gaily, "If there is a girl among you belonging to the year of the rat, the rest of you are qualified to act as middlemen. But if there is no one belonging to the year of the rat please do not bother to discuss the matter!" So no one who did not belong to the year of the rat would ever be considered.

My mother was also a very determined woman. Once she had decided that something was right, or if she had set her heart on it, she would allow nothing to turn her aside. From beginning to end she was totally unbending.

This girl had been introduced to her by a relative, who had been a baptized church member for more than ten years. Yet in this matter he gravely erred and acted in a way plainly displeasing to God. Having traced a girl born in the year of the rat he arranged for my mother to accompany him in a visit to a fortune-teller. Naturally the blind fortune-teller used so many auspicious words that my mother permitted herself a beaming smile and clapped her hands several times as if striking a gong. In her eyes nothing now remained but for me to marry the girl. Yet according to my own enquiries she was totally unsuitable; she was an unbeliever.

On the evening that they returned, after consulting the fortune-teller, my mother said, "The blind gentleman assured us that the arrangement was ideal, and that after your marriage everything in the home would run smoothly."

I couldn't help laughing and I asked my mother, "What is it to do with me that the blind gentleman says all will be well?"

My mother stubbornly replied, "I am the head in this matter. Within the next few months the engagement will be completed and you will be married in January next year."

I said, "Don't let us be in such a hurry. Let us go carefully into the whole situation!" She would not change her mind, however, and insisted that I indicate my approval immediately. Without another word she then went outside, and did not return. I made enquiries everywhere among relatives and friends, but I could not find her anywhere.

My mother did not return for three days. When she did her face was the picture of misery and she appeared to be overwhelmed by bitter grief. That evening, when I returned home for my meal, she pressed me again to agree to the arrangement. "Mother!" I said, "I cannot agree." As soon as she heard this her tears began to flow. She gave vent to her feelings and began to cry out loudly, jumping about as if she was out of her mind. There appeared to be no way to quieten her. But it was already time for the evening meeting that I was to lead, so I could only do my best to comfort her before going out.

Gloomy indeed was our home. The next few months passed in an atmosphere of melancholy and grief. Even when my mother was not openly crying her tears were flowing. Her heart was filled with inexpressible sorrow, and my own heart was full of bitter suffering. I was sleeping in the church building at that time but I always returned home for my evening meal. Every evening I returned home with apprehension and trembling. I did not stay there long lest I further arouse my mother's feelings and add to her suffering. So I always finished my meal as quickly as I could and went out.

One evening, when we were eating our evening meal together, my mother suddenly said to me "If you don't give your approval this evening I will die in front of you!" What an alarming situation! Having uttered this threat she then began to roll backwards and forwards on the couch, crying and shouting all the time. I did everything I possibly could but I still could not pacify her. Sometimes she would kneel down and bump her head on the floor. It was as if my heart was pierced by a sword. When I did not immediately reply she wanted to go on banging her head on the floor and die. My strength was exhausted. Where would I find a remedy? I could only continue praying to the Lord.

At that juncture I was feeling more and more that unless the Lord increased my strength I would be forced to give way. How could I be other than overwhelmed with grief to see my mother in such a state? So I said to her, "Mother! What about my waiting for three years and then marrying the girl?" I knew that unless I gave some sort of reply my mother would not have allowed me to go out, and I had to lead a special meeting that evening.

She replied, "A year at the most!"

While I was conducting the meeting I frequently lifted my heart to the Lord, calling upon Him fervently to add to my strength and to show me the way. I knew that God wanted me to spend my life in preaching the gospel, so that men and women might be saved, but if I contracted the marriage that my mother wanted how would that be possible?

On returning to Shanghai I again said to my mother, "I know that all you do arises out of your love for your son, but I do not want..." As soon as I reached the words "do not want" my mother began to cry again. But since an evangelistic meeting was scheduled that evening and time was already pressing, I could only contain the grief in my heart and go out to undertake my ministry.

That evening, while I was preaching the gospel, my heart was full of sorrow, and in view of my mother's condition my mind was far from easy. So I asked my fellow-workers to go and enquire how my mother was. The reply indicated that so far all was well. Even so I could not sleep, and kept calling on the Lord to preserve my mother's life and to keep her from anything untoward.

In the midst of all this bitter suffering who was there to give comfort and sympathy? Only the Lord. In the midst of my pain and sorrow the Lord drew out my heart in love for Him. He was my only hope and deliverer. He only could enable me to overcome.

Although my mother continued to put pressure on me, the basic reason for my refusal was the fact that this girl was not a Christian believer. It could not therefore be God's will. But because of my inability to agree, my mother was again roused to the point of wailing and creating disturbances.

The hour of deliverance was now at hand. Thanks be to God, it was He who opened a way of escape. The situation that had arisen in our home, and the conflict between my mother and myself, were in time made known to the other family concerned. The head of the girl's family then stated: "Since the woman's son is unwilling for the match, why should we give our daughter to him in marriage?" Thanks be to the Lord!

Another factor also weighed with the girl's family. The fact that I was "one who preaches Jesus" raised a question, in that they were people who worshipped their ancestors. Because of this they were even more unwilling to go ahead with plans for the proposed match. This news was relayed to me because throughout the period of uncertainty I had sent someone regularly to get news of that family. In fact their attitude was something I had been praying about daily.

I was naturally elated to hear this news, and went

off to inform my mother. But when she saw my
smiling face and my exuberant manner she realized
what had happened and her face fell. She relapsed
into absolute silence. "Mother!" I said, "This report
is true. Please don't blame me. The girl's family have
discussed the situation and they have come to the
conclusion that they do not wish to go ahead with
the proposed arrangement. Someone has come from
their home in the country to bring us the news."

She listened to these words and then began to wail
in a loud voice, knocking her head against the wall.
All she could think of was death. I comforted her
and pointed out that the decision meant we were left
with no alternative. "This is a true report," I
repeated. "Never have I told you a lie and this you
know."

When I went back home the following evening I
found that my mother was still very displeased with
me. She thought that these recent developments
were due to collusion between me and the members
of the girl's family. My mother felt that she had
fallen just short of success [lit. by one basket of earth
as when making a mound]. She blamed me for the
obstruction.

This period of testing lasted for more than ten
months and was certainly the greatest test I had
experienced. The bitterness of that period so entered
into my being that it will remain engraved on my
heart for the rest of my life. I was upheld throughout
the whole period, however, by the prayer of several
devoted brothers and sisters in the Lord. This is
what gave me the strength to overcome adverse
circumstances and for this I give thanks and praise to
God.

It so happened that on January 18 Shanghai was

engulfed in fighting, and as a consequence of this one phase of my marriage experiences was brought to a close.

But there is one element that I must comment on. It concerns my relative — a church member — who accompanied my mother to the fortune-teller. Through sinning in this way he caused immense harm to my mother and brought her much suffering. Not long afterwards, unfortunately, this relative became seriously ill, and had to have brain surgery. The wound became infected and his face changed colour. My mother wished me to visit him in hospital, and when I did so he wanted me to pray for him. Constrained by the love of Christ, I overcame my personal feelings and poured out my heart for him.

Although my relative was not my enemy, it was he who had taken the initiative in introducing this girl to my mother and who had urged my mother to go to the fortune-teller. In so doing he became responsible for those months of misery. Yet when I saw him so ill I remembered God's righteousness and my heart was filled with God's love. I pleaded for him fervently with my whole heart. At the end of my prayer I said, "Amen!" and he also said "Amen!" I sang a hymn and he also sang a hymn. For years he had never opened his mouth to praise God but now that he was in trouble he revealed the love for the Lord which had long been buried in his heart.

While my relative was still in hospital I visited him again, and my mother and another relative happened to visit him at the same time. While we were there a reference was made to my future. My visiting relative addressed himself to my mother: "As for Shiguang," he said, "Let him work things out for himself. Why need you interfere?" My mother was silent and so was my relative in the hospital bed. It seemed to me that they were both of the same opinion.

I had now gained a measure of freedom, but that freedom was not absolute. My mother still advocated that when I was eventually married I should first go and worship ceremonially at the shrine, and only after that go to the church for the actual wedding ceremony. So hindrances and problems still remained. To anticipate for a moment, when the time eventually came God worked things out for me. And my mother made none of the stubborn demands that had been threatened.

For three or four years I regularly prayed to God about "the great affair of a lifetime." God then undertook. Prior to that time I had had no close affinity with the one who is now my wife. We had never even come face to face and had certainly never been friends. But when once a move was made everything happened quickly. On June 18th last year we were engaged and on July 9th we were married. Actually several elderly people had first made enquiries and God opened the way. My mother raised no obstacle whatever. We were most clearly guided by the Lord. Now we two comfort each other and help each other. Humbly and gratefully we travel together the path of life. Trusting in the Lord's great power and might we dedicate ourselves to fight together under the banner of the Lord. Amen!

FINALLY

They hear -but do they heed?

Wang Mingdao
Ezekiel 33:30-33

SOME CHRISTIANS attend a place of worship only rarely, or never. We generally regard them as backsliders. There are of course legitimate reasons for Christians not attending a place of worship: a believer may be physically ill, or hindered by duties, or prevented by other circumstances beyond his control. But apart from this, if he fails to go to a place of worship, he has either been drawn away by love of the world, or become unconcerned about drawing near to God, or has fallen into sin and is ashamed to face God or His people.

We can turn this line of reasoning around and say that all Christians who regularly attend a place of worship are devout and zealous believers. For the majority this would be valid, but the facts tell us that many Christians who attend a place of worship are neither devout nor zealous. A similar situation was found among the Israelites of old.

In this passage of Scripture we can see how God spoke to His servant Ezekiel about the Israelites. He described how they diligently assembled together, how they delighted to listen to the prophet's preaching, and how they talked about him "by the walls and at the doors of the houses". They were undoubtedly eulogizing Ezekiel for the way he preached. They would describe his appropriate illustrations and his fluent words. One would say to another, "Come and hear the message that has come from the Lord." All this is plain evidence that they delighted to listen to a message from God and were zealous to serve Him. They also made their way to the place where the prophet was, not in dribbles but in droves, and sat before him to listen to his words.

They certainly gave the impression that they were devout people of God. But that is not the whole story. They are described as people who "listen to your words, but do not put them into practice." Previously we could only admire them, yet this sentence injects a feeling of doubt. And that is not all. "With their mouths they express devotion, but their hearts are greedy for unjust gain." Ah! What a comedown! A few words spoil everything. Who would have thought it? These people who assembled zealously together and listened attentively to the message, were all the time "greedy for unjust gain."

It is only when we read the next words that we understand the significance of this. The people are delighted to listen to the message, but not with a view to putting it into practice. They look on the prophet as "nothing more than one who sings love songs with a beautiful voice and plays an instrument well." In other words, they did not listen attentively to the message in order to receive spiritual benefit, nor to be instructed in the right way to live. They listened solely to satisfy their ears. What drew them was Ezekiel's manner of speech and articulate delivery. With his silver-tongued eloquence he could stir their emotions. And in the same way as it delighted them to listen attentively to a beautiful singer or instrumentalist, so it delighted them to listen to Ezekiel delivering a message from the Lord. It is not surprising that such people do not put the message into practice.

When people listen to a message simply because it gives pleasure to their ears, it is natural that they do not make spiritual progress. Nevertheless the time is not entirely wasted. At the very least they momentarily experience the pleasure of listening. They also share with other people the fact that they go constantly and listen to the prophet, and thus give the impression that this is an enjoyable exercise for them.

But all is not well. By doing this they can also provoke disaster. "When all this comes true — and it surely will — then they will know that a prophet has been among them." What is it that will surely come true? At this point we should read verses 27-29:

"Say this to them, 'This is what the Sovereign Lord says: As surely as I live, those who are left in the ruins will fall by the sword, those out in the country I will give to the wild animals to be devoured, and those in strongholds and caves will die of a plague. I will make the land a desolate waste, and her proud strength will come to an end, and the mountains of Israel will become desolate so that no one will cross them. Then they will know that I am the Lord, when I have made the land a desolate waste because of all the detestable things they have done.'"

God's purpose in speaking through the prophet of these impending disasters was not that He might make them come to pass, but rather that they might *not* come to pass. What God hoped with all His heart was that when the people of Israel heard these words they would accept the warning and quickly repent. Then all that He had spoken about the onset of calamity would come to nothing, as Jonah's preaching to the Ninevites did. If the people of Israel listened sincerely to Ezekiel's preaching and also obeyed God, then God would surely turn aside the threatened disaster.

Alas! Although they assembled in the presence of the prophet and were willing to listen to him preaching, they got no further. They did not put into practice what they had heard. So in the end the disaster that the Lord had spoken about came upon them.

This state of affairs also occurs today. Among those who regularly attend meetings, are there some who eagerly listen to the voice of the preacher and yet do not put into practice what they hear? "By the walls and at the doors of the houses" they discuss the ability of particular preachers. They call to each other, "Come and hear the message that has come from the Lord!" They make their way to a place of worship and sit down like devout believers. But they make no change whatever in their manner of life. The preacher may denounce their sins but the people do not renounce them. They make no attempt to do what the preacher teaches. Those who have been in the habit of telling untruths continue to lie. Those who have given way to envy continue to envy. Those who have been in the habit of self-seeking continue to be self-seeking. Those who have been covetous continue to covet.

At the time of meeting together they seem to be as

holy as angels, but in their everyday lives they can become as wicked as demons. The pattern they exhibit at church is one thing; the pattern they exhibit at home or in their social life is quite different. When people of this character attend meetings it is not for the purpose of worshipping God, to learn how to please Him or how to do His will. They meet simply because it is their custom to do so. They eagerly listen to the message, but only because the preacher preaches in an interesting way and his eloquence satisfies their ears. Or perhaps they listen to the message in order to advance their knowledge of the Bible and their intellectual understanding of spiritual truths. That not only satisfies their thirst for knowledge but also gives them something to discuss. They appear to be devout Christians. But when they listen to the sermon it is exactly like listening to beautiful singing and playing, and their manner of life is no more affected than it would be by that.

God tells us that this was the attitude of the Israelites; the facts tell us that this is the attitude of many church-goers today. So we may be quite wrong when we describe all those who attend meetings and listen to the message as devout Christians.

Is there any benefit to be gained from attending meetings and listening to the message in such a frame of mind? No. Far from being profitable, it is actually harmful. If we listen to a message in such a frame of mind we can never receive God's blessing. For we shall be no different from the Israelites of whom it is written, "With their mouths they express devotion, but their hearts are greedy for unjust gain."

It is not only among the listeners that people like

this are to be found. Preachers can show similar characteristics. The prophet Micah said: "[Israel's] leaders judge for a bribe, her priests teach for a price, and her prophets tell fortunes for money. Yet they lean upon the Lord and say, 'Is not the Lord among us? No disaster will come upon us'" (Micah 3:11).

If this was common in Israel of old, it is also common in the church today. It is not the truth of God that preachers are preaching, but the theories of the world. This does not only apply to those who are openly leading people along the path of error. Even among preachers who profess to preach the true gospel, many seek merely to please men and do not preach the whole counsel of God. In their sermons they do not give full value; they are underweight. Not a few preachers are engaged in preaching only to fill their food-bowl; their eyes are on remuneration or reputation. Since they are not faithfully proclaiming the word of God they dare not reprove sin nor point out the things that God condemns. All that they can do is to preach sermons in a manner comparable to singing beautiful songs and playing on musical instruments. They give pleasure to the ear — but no more. They may even preach didactic sermons and thus add to people's store of knowledge. But that is just an intellectual exercise. There are other preachers for whom preaching is simply a pretext, a cover-up for shady practices. All these activities are of the flesh. How can they be profitable spiritually?

The words of Ezekiel, then, contain warnings for both listeners and preachers. Are you among those believers of whom it can be said that "with their mouths they express devotion, but their hearts are greedy for unjust gain"? Are you among those who listen to a preacher's words but "do not put them into practice"? If so, you must quickly repent if you would escape God's judgement.

And you preachers, who "teach for a price" and "tell fortunes for money"! You too ought to repent without delay. For otherwise an even greater judgement will come upon you!

Biographical Notes

Wang Mingdao

Mr Wang Mingdao may be regarded as one of the three most outstanding and influential evangelical preachers and leaders in China in this century (the others being Dr John Sung and Watchman Nee). Mr Wang established the Christians' Tabernacle in Peking where he ministered to a large congregation. At the same time he was in great demand as a speaker, and spent roughly six months each year as the special speaker at Conventions and evangelistic meetings throughout China. He also edited a magazine entitled *Spiritual Food Quarterly*, for which he provided most of the material. After 1949 Mr Wang spent 23 years in prison — his wife 20 years — because of their allegiance to Christ and their faithful testimony. At the age of 87 he and his wife now live in retirement in Shanghai.

John Sung

Dr John Sung has been described as "the greatest evangelist China has ever known. Although possessing brilliant academic qualifications, he nevertheless at the call of God turned wholly to the work of preaching the gospel"[1] John Sung was born in the province of Fujian in Southeast China and died in Peking in 1944 at the early age of 42. During the fifteen years of his active ministry he travelled widely, visiting overseas Chinese in many countries of Southeast Asia, as well as preaching in centres all over China. His messages now in print were mostly recorded from his preaching ministry, and thus are characterized by a spoken rather than a literary style. If ever a man burned out for God it was Dr John Sung.

Marcus Cheng

The ministry of the Rev Marcus Cheng was one of ever-widening circles. The early spiritual influences in his life were due to the work of Swedish missionaries, and for a while he taught in a Bible School in the province of Hunan. When he later undertook wider ministry he paid several visits to Sweden. He was invited to be a speaker at well-known conventions not only in Sweden, but also in the United Kingdom, the United States, and in a number of other countries. He wrote in all more than forty books and was the editor of the magazine *Evangelism* which he had helped to establish. After the war he accepted the invitation of the CIM General Director to cooperate in the opening of Chongqing Theological Seminary, where he served as Principal until political changes brought about the closure of all such Christian institutions and activities.

David Yang

David Yang grew up in the northern province of Shanxi, where he was early recognized by the CIM-related churches not only as an acceptable speaker but also as a Christian leader with unusual spiritual insight. Before the war with Japan he had founded the "Spiritual Work Team" — a group of young people who gathered for study and training during the period when farmers were busy and scattered for ministry when farmers were slack. After the war his ministry was extended to areas far from the province of Shanxi, including Peking, Nanking, and Shanghai. He was the author of several books, such as *The Church and Worker*, and when the Communists came to power he was editing a useful publication entitled *The Spiritual Work Newsletter*.

Wilson Wang

Wilson Wang was the younger brother of the better known Leland Wang (Wang Zai) and a classmate of the young man who became known as Watchman Nee. The two families were neighbours on a hillside in the suburbs of Fuzhou. Leland Wang had already qualified as a naval officer and Wilson Wang was a student at Canton naval school, but both brothers gave up their careers to become preachers of the gospel. At first they were closely associated with Watchman Nee in evangelistic work (hence the message by Wilson Wang is taken from a magazine, *The Christian*, then edited by Watchman Nee), but the brothers decided to separate from Mr Nee and they then pursued independent preaching ministries. I heard Wilson Wang when he preached at a Chinese Church in Tokyo in the late 1950s.

C K Cheng

The Rev C K Cheng was at one time a member of the staff of Hunan Bible Institute in Changsha. He later became known as a convention speaker, a collection of his messages being published by his friends after his death in 1940.

Min Ruji

Min Ruji, who exercised a preaching ministry in the Shanghai area at a time of unrest, was associated with David Yang in the publication of the monthly *Spiritual Work Newsletter*.

---

1 *Flame for God*, the biography of John Sung by Leslie Lyall, (OMF Books).